How to create an Affiliate program from scratch and grow it – *in 5 proven steps!*

Looking to launch your own Affiliate program? This book explains in 5 proven steps, how to create it from scratch and grow it.

AF595985

With over 15 years of experience in growing affiliate programs from scratch, I have worked with multiple businesses and established this proven 5 step method.

My expertise lies in working particularly with start-ups and creating and setting up affiliate channels from scratch, and growing it to becoming their highest performing digital channel.

This method is proven time and time again with businesses that have gone on perform rapid growth and exceed targets. With the affiliate channel to thank for their explosive growth.

Lets now delve into the 5 proven steps to creating an affiliate program for your business...

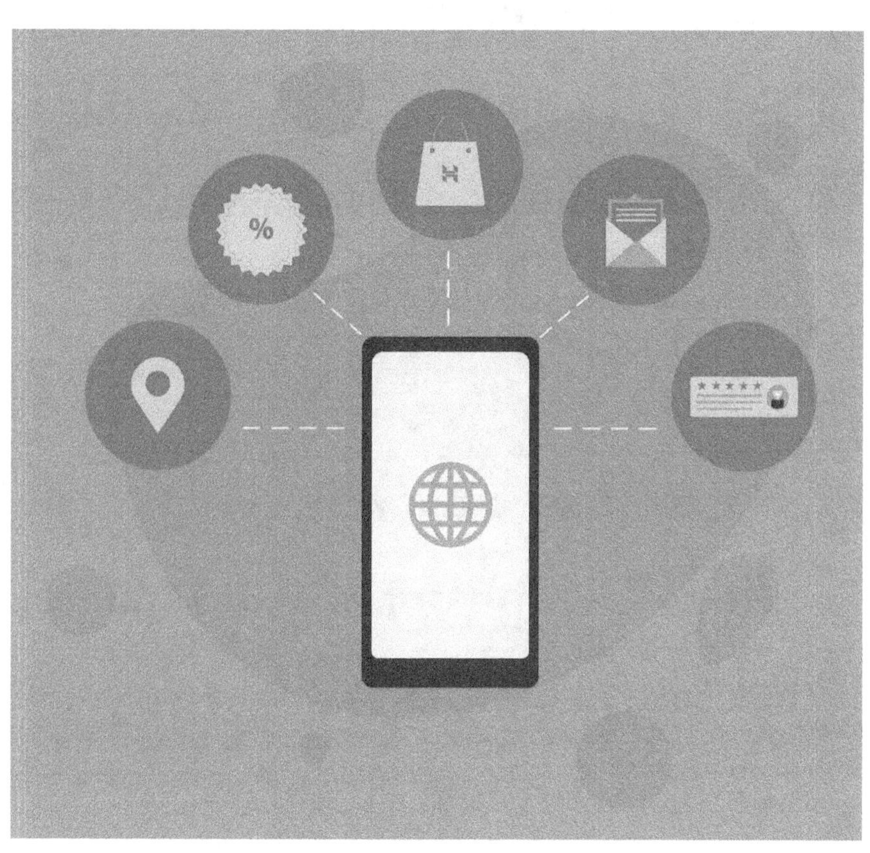

Content: What this book will cover

This book will cover the 5 proven steps to creating

your affiliate channel from scratch...

1. **Introduction: The role of the Affiliate Channel**
2. **Step 1: Research**
3. **Step 2: Build**
4. **Step 3: Agencies & Networks**
5. **Step 4: Recruitment**
6. **Step 5: Growth**
7. **Big-name brands who've successfully grown their business using superior affiliate programs**
8. **Ongoing Affiliate Strategy**

Introduction: The role of the Affiliate Channel

Before we go straight into the 5 steps, let's take a step back and look at the role of the affiliate channel. It's important to understand and establish this so that there's sufficient background knowledge of the channel and how it works, before research, build and growth can occur.

What is the role of the affiliate channel going to be in your business?

As the image below describes, it is one of the earliest forms of digital marketing. Since the dawn of the internet, sites have asked other sites whether they will promote them. It therefore sits within the big 4 of paid digital marketing; alongside Display, PPC and Social.

The role of the Affiliate channel

One of, if not the earliest, form of Digital Marketing

Considered the conversion end of the customer funnel. If PPC is considered awareness then affiliates is often the last stage where the conversion happens

Most consider Digital Marketing to be the big 4: PPC, Display, Social Media and Affiliates

As one of the big 4, these are often labelled Performance Marketing channels, due to their directly relatable tracking

Within advertisers you'll often find one member to an entire dedicated team, sitting within Digital Marketing, focusing on affiliate marketing

Unlike the other Big 4 channels, affiliate marketing is unique in such as you only pay for conversions. Whereas in Display you pay for impressions, PPC for clicks, and Social for either.

For affiliate marketing, in most cases you pay per conversion or completed sale. It is therefore the last remaining and true performance channel.

It's the very reason that almost every major brand still utilises affiliate marketing in some format. Whether that's a full-blown affiliate program, or simply a handful of partnerships.

Affiliates, those that promote your brand to their audience, can often be split into incentivised vs non-incentivised.

Those who are 'incentivised' include an offer, discount, or cashback sites. Sites such as *Topcashback* and *Quidco* in the U.K. are some of the largest cashback sites with 10m+ members.

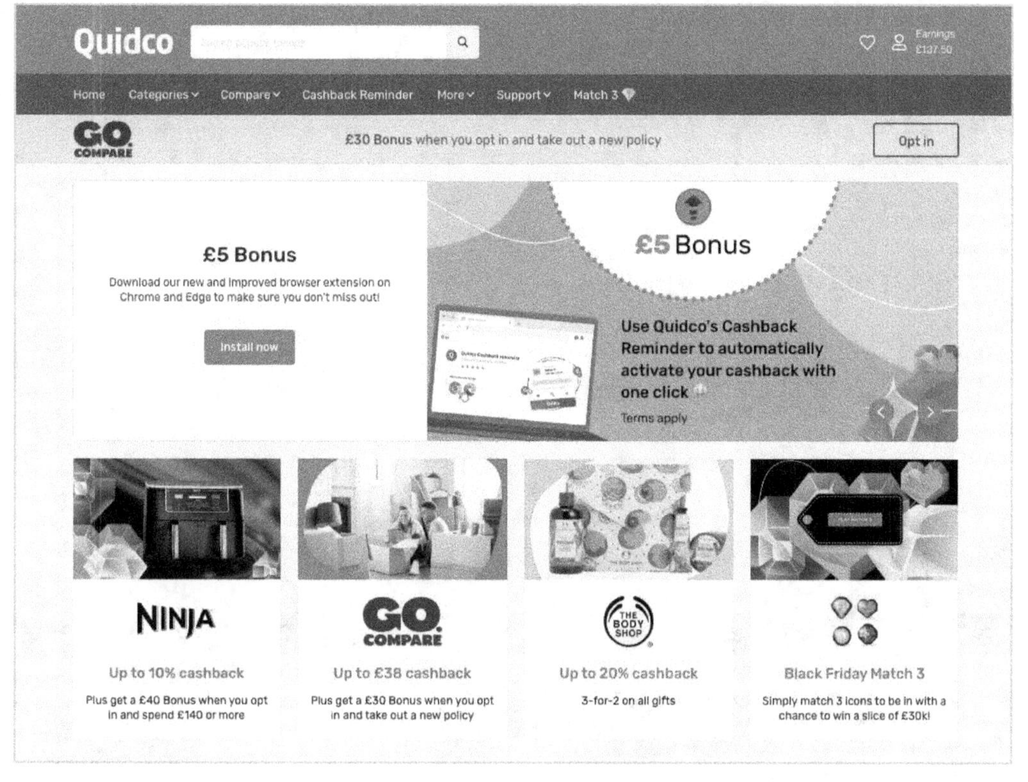

There are also voucher sites like *VoucherCodes* or *MyVoucherCodes*, demographic specific discount sites like *Kidstart* who focus on children offers or *Easyfundraising* which is charitable.

'Non-incentivised' can include offers and discounts, but that's not why they exist. Often they're meant for informative reasons, such as advise, comparison or reviews.

These include *Moneysavingexpert*, the largest money saving portal in the U.K. with 15m+ members.

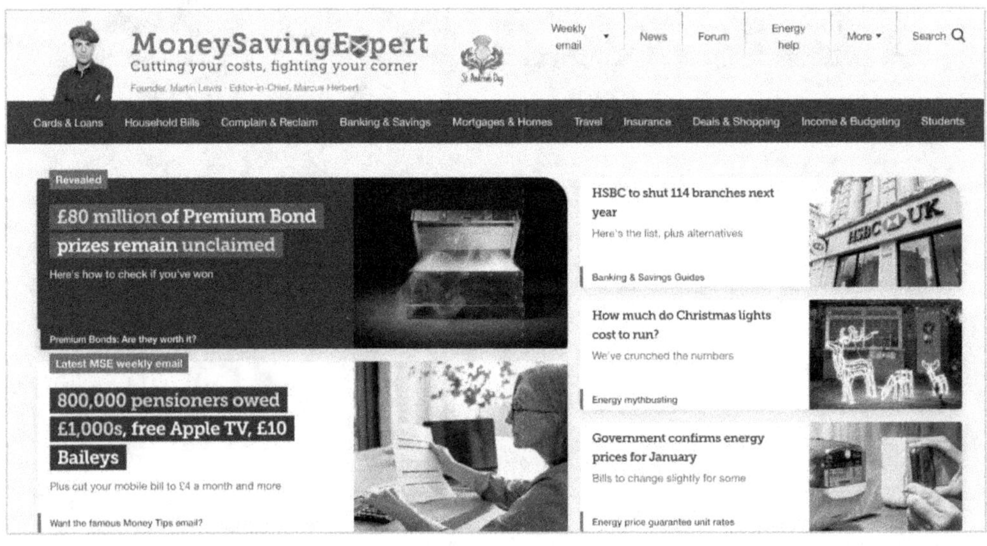

There are large comparison sites such as *GoCompare*, *Compare the market*, or niche comparison such as *BroadbandChoices* who focus purely on broadband comparison.

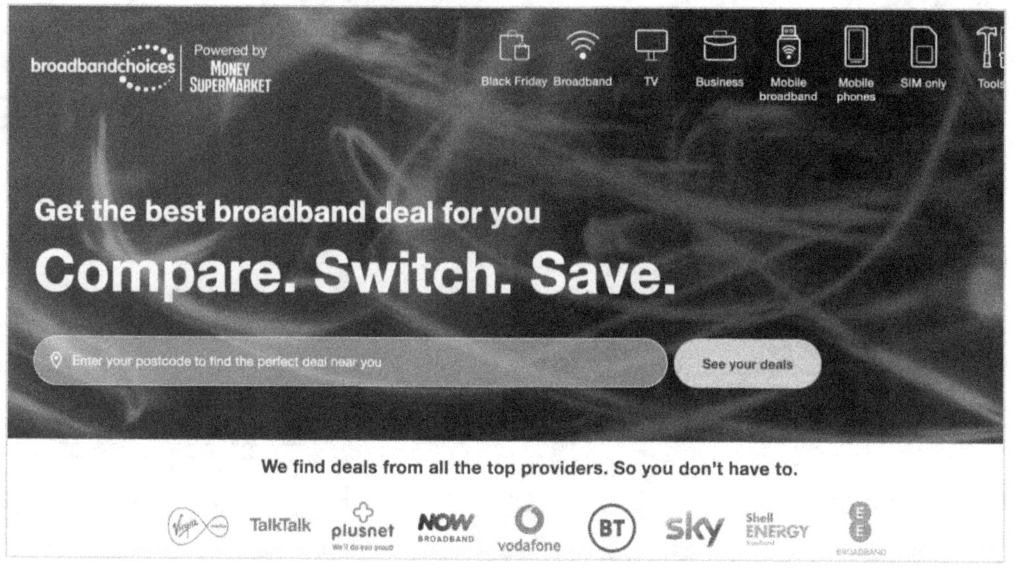

There are also content publishers like *Lovemoney* and *ThisIsMoney*, or fan enthusiasts sites like *DriveTribe* for car fans.

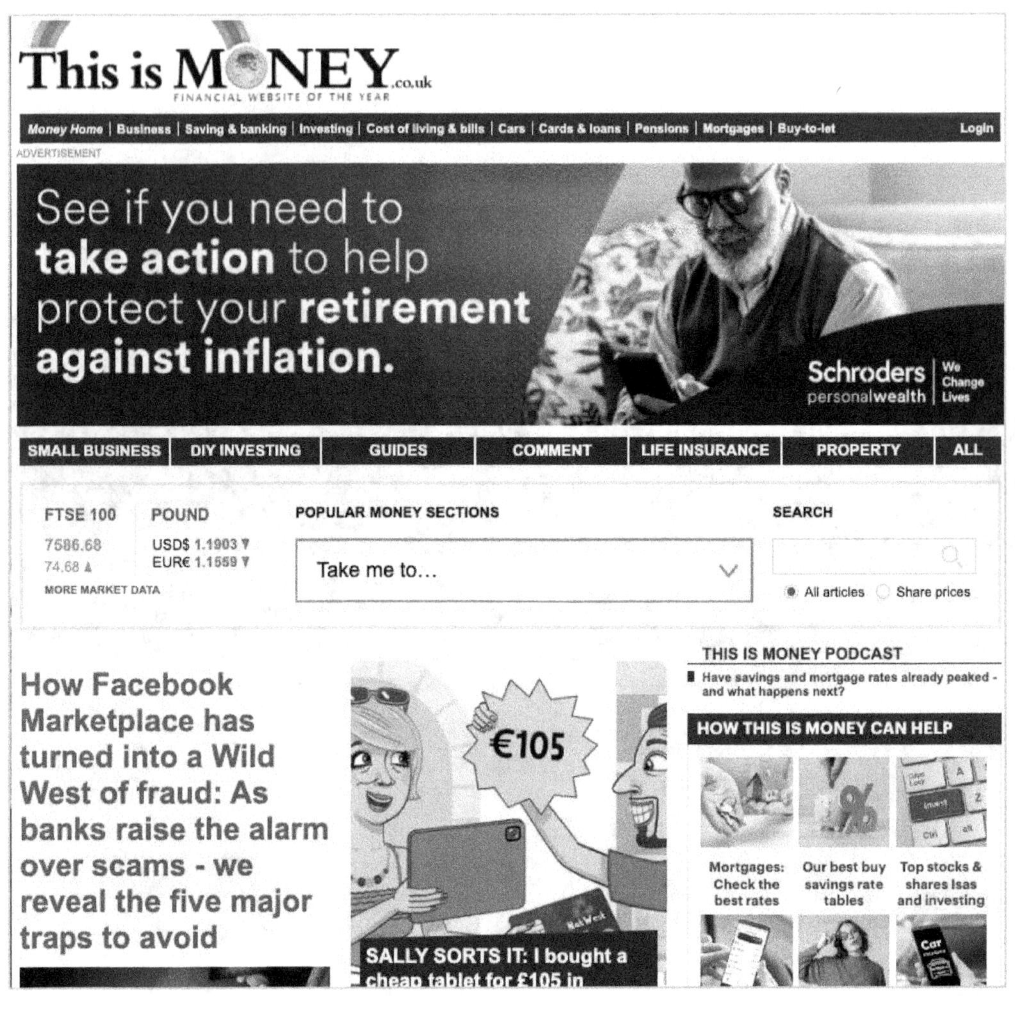

Within these sites, which within the industry are generally called 'publishers', there is a whole range of possible advertising placements for your brand.

Depending on the level of control within your affiliate program, the publisher will place you on their site via a text link, whole article, widget or banner, email or within their comparison table. This level of exposure is where you'll engage with their audience and encourage them to click through to your site to make the sale.

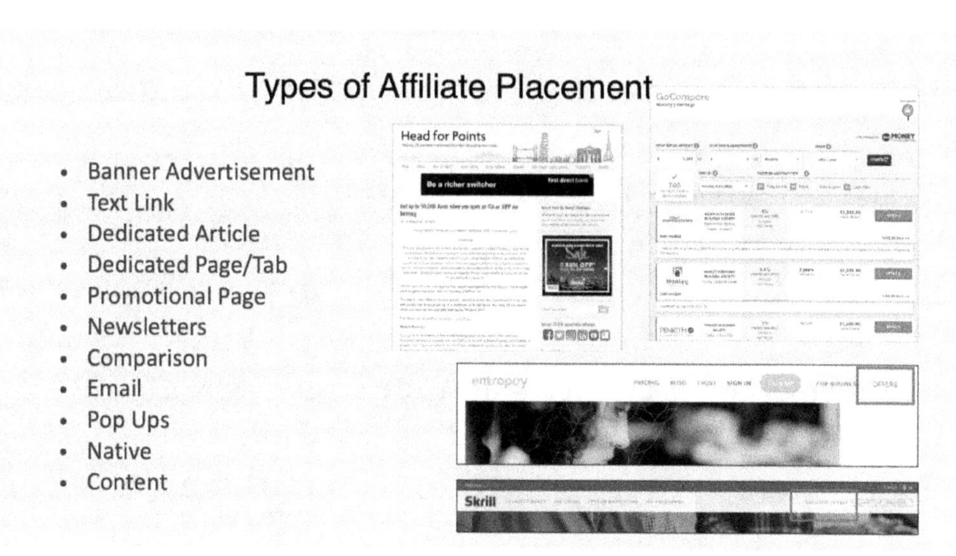

Step 1: Research

The first step to creating your affiliate program is to research.

This means asking yourself two questions — is there an appetite for affiliate marketing internally in your organisation and an appetite in my industry .i.e. are there publishers out there? And secondly, what are my competitors doing in the space?

Below are further considerations and a thought process to go through when it comes to your research. You should establish what you're willing to pay for each sale in terms of a CPA, you should see if this is competitive enough versus your competition. From there you should start to determine your objectives with your channel, which for most will be purely acquisition. Although it can also be a branding and retention play.

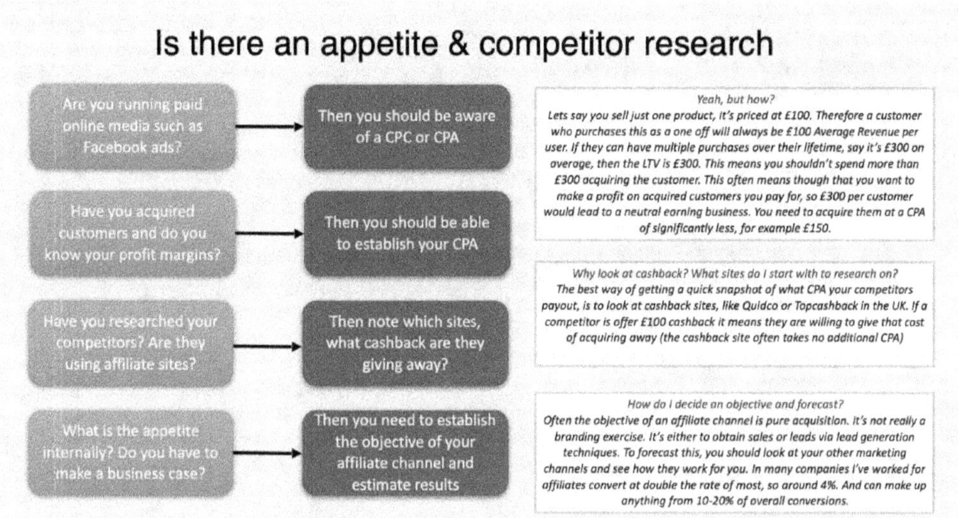

Step 2: Build

Moving onto the build phase, you first need to gather various elements of your affiliate program before you can start to reach out to potential publishers. Below is a list of these items you need, and we'll delve into most of them over the next slides.

Starting from scratch – what you need

So, lets assume you're starting from nothing...no 3rd party websites are promoting you and your digital presence is next to nothing...how do you start from scratch?

Even if you're a client-side affiliate manager who's used to a 1,000+ publisher base for a big brand it's important to understand where how foundations of an affiliate channel form.

- Competitor & industry research
- Establish whether there is demand and appetite in your company – get all stakeholders on-board
- Establish your LTV & CPA and a range of commission options
- Create an affiliate map – to understand potential publishers
- Ensure Google Analytics is set up with relevant default & custom channel grouping and event tracking
- Write your affiliate program terms and conditions
- Create a page on your website (/affiliates) with basic information about what it means to partner
- Create an email template and/or deck to send to publishers
- Register to a network (longer process, so can wait until later) and agree terms – create your advertiser page

These items are required for those who are building their affiliate channel completely from scratch. As mentioned below it assumes you have no third-party sites promoting you yet, and you're a start-up with some but not a lot of digital presence.

One of the first items to consider is tracking. How are you going to record a visit and conversion from a customer coming from your partner's site to your own?

We go onto mention how affiliate networks can aid this step, but even prior to working with them, the cheaper and frankly easier way is to utilise Google. Assuming you have Google Analytics set up, as well, goals and events in place, you can create your affiliate links simply by adding your UTM string to your URL.

As described below you simply need to add the name of the affiliate to your 'source' and 'affiliates' to your 'medium'. Once the link is used by a partner site, customers coming through will appear under the 'affiliates' default channel group, and you'll know the conversions at each stage of your funnel. You should then have your 'revenue' set up as a column to record how much you're earning off each partner.

This can also be utilised to work out the commission you should pay them, but making a custom column and attributing a revenue share or CPA to each sale. More on this below.

From there you can make a Google Data Studio dashboard to use as your affiliate report with the partner. Again, more on this below.

What we're trying to say is, Google has such free tools to get you started. You don't need an affiliate network or Saas technology from the beginning.

Basic Tracking

- Any website can have basic affiliate tracking by simply using Google Analytics. Make sure GA is set up for your business.
- Step 2 is to check you have default channel groups set up so that on your reports 'Affiliates' will show.
- It will show if you provide your affiliates the following UTM code, this follows the end of your website as follows...

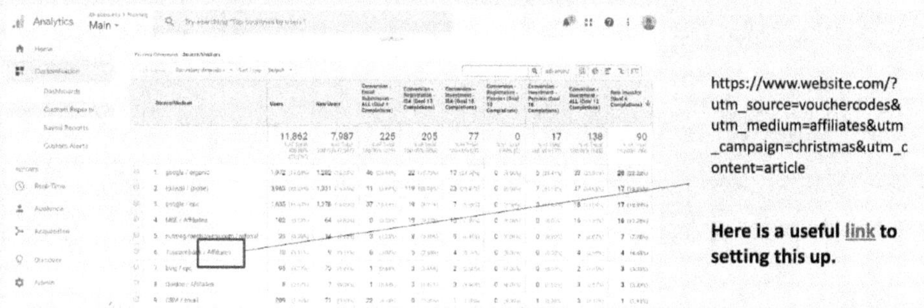

Below describes how to set up the UTM tracking in even more detail. You can even utilise the 'campaign' and 'content' UTM's to further track what links customers are coming from into your funnel.

In-House / Client-Side Tracking

All advertisers can utilise the most basic UTM tracking through to Google Analytics to run their affiliate program, it works like this...

https://www.udemy.com/isas?utm_source=vouchercodes&utm_medium=affiliates&utm_campaign=christmas&utm_content=article

- *utm_source=vouchercodes*
- *utm_medium=affiliates*
- *utm_campaign=christmas*
- *utm_content=article*

Next you need to build your Google Data Studio reports. This will allow each partner to see their performance in real-time. Again, it's free to create these for your partners, and means you don't need a complicated SaaS tool to begin with — until you grow your channel to a considerable size.

If you're familiar with the Google suite you will see alongside Google Docs, Google Data Studio. This platform allows you to create visually stunning dashboards with very little effort.

Starting with a blank slate you need to connect your Google Analytics data to your Google Data Studio. This is a relatively simple process as Google guides you through it. And as your Google Analytics is most likely connected through the same account the data should pull through.

Next it's a case of creating models in the dashboard itself. This can be done by selecting graphs, text boxes, or tables. Once inserted it will pull through your whole Google Analytics data for your entire site. You now just need to filter the tables and graphs to your medium, which will be 'affiliate'. This means it will now only show all of your affiliate data.

You can further segment the data by asking Data Studio to simply show you source, and the source name, which will be the name of the affiliate. In our example it's '*lovemoney*'. This will then show all of *Lovemoney's* results.

Assuming you have goals set up in Google Analytics. You can now pull through the relevant conversion data, and show Lovemoney's clicks, leads and sales. And suddenly you have a completed reporting dashboard for them.

Add in some visuals, such as titles and their logo, and restrict the logins to just Lovemoney users. Now you can share the dashboard with the partner. As Google Analytics works in near real-time, they can simply login any time they wish to view their performance. In this way it acts exactly like a SaaS solution or affiliate network program would, but for free!

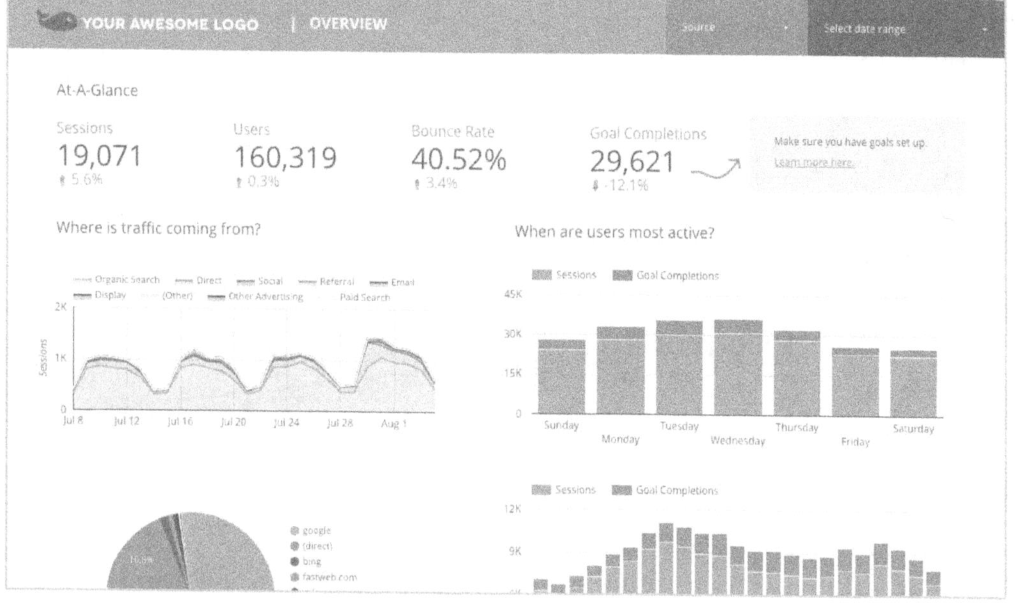

Next it's time to move away from tracking and dashboards to prepare your content.

The reason we do this now is to have your articles, banners and co-branded landing pages all ready to distribute to affiliates. This way they can simply go ahead and start promoting you, without any delay. You're also doing the leg work for them here.

With affiliate marketing you want to make it as easy as possible for a third party site to promote you. By already doing the heavy lifting for them, all they have to do to refer customers is grab your banner and paste it onto your site.

Prepare your creatives & content

It might be curious to you why create your ads and content now...well here is why...

- You can't start to reach out to your publishers without something for them to promote
- You can't go, 'hey here is my great website and products for you to promote' without something for them to put on their website or something useful for them to link to

Let's remember...

Publishers are selling for you
So, give them the tools to sell...

Creatives

- Make a range of ads in all IAB recommended sizes
- Consider include an exclusive offer
- Create your brand guidelines – more on this later

Content

- Some affiliates only promote a small paragraph explaining who you are, so have this written in your best light. Some may only give you a matter of words.
- What are your terms – other affiliates have an offer of yours, like cashback, so make sure you know what rules are set
- Landing pages – it's not just about what they write about you, its also what they link to. Make sure your pages are as strong as they can be

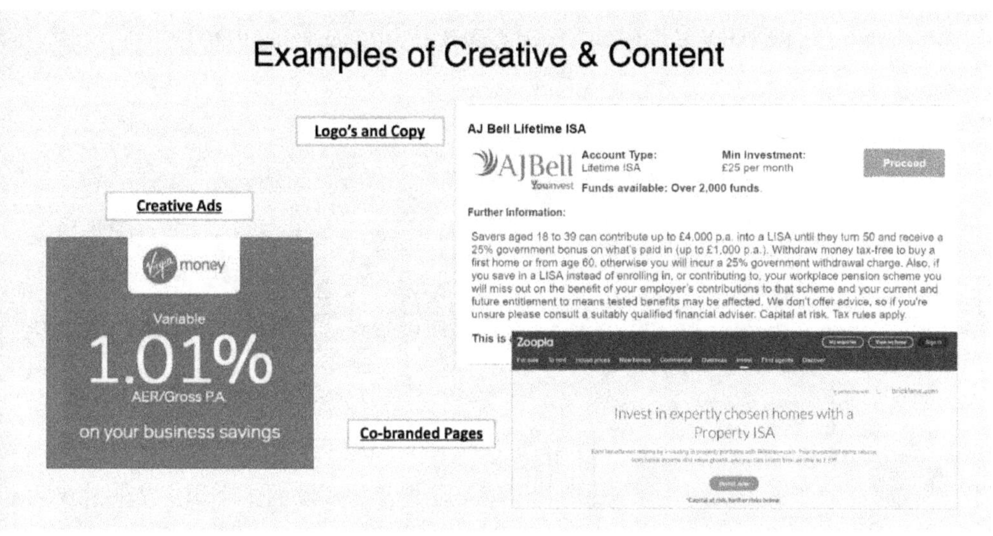

The build must continue with additional elements, aside from the important tracking and creative/content pieces.

You will need to establish your commission structures (explained in detail later), how invoicing and payment will work, contracts and whether you will use them, and a brand guidelines document, to keep all affiliates in check when it comes to using/misuse of your brand.

A key part of your affiliate program build is to create a simple sign up page. Commonly affiliate programs will have a detailed page of how to sign up to your program, all the benefits of why you should promote your brand, a link to the terms and conditions and commission structures.

As we go onto explain, affiliate networks house this piece for you, and if you search most affiliate program for popular brands you will find their dedicated page on the likes of *Awin* and *Rakuten*.

Starting from scratch though, particularly if you are a start-up, you don't necessarily have to sign up to an affiliate program to create this page.

Many businesses make a simple sign-up form on their own website to begin with. Often this is the best way, saving you having to work and pay an affiliate network, or use third-party in-house affiliate software.

All you need to begin with is a simple sign up form, or better yet an email address on a splash page, so publishers can write in if they wish to join. For now, while you have no affiliate partners, this is the easy recommended approach, until you can advance it later on.

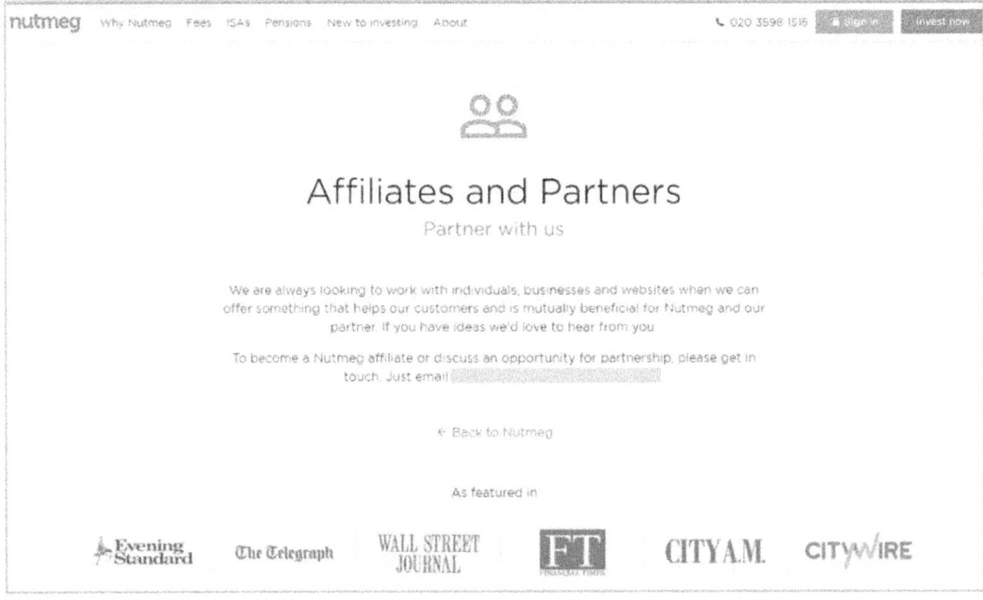

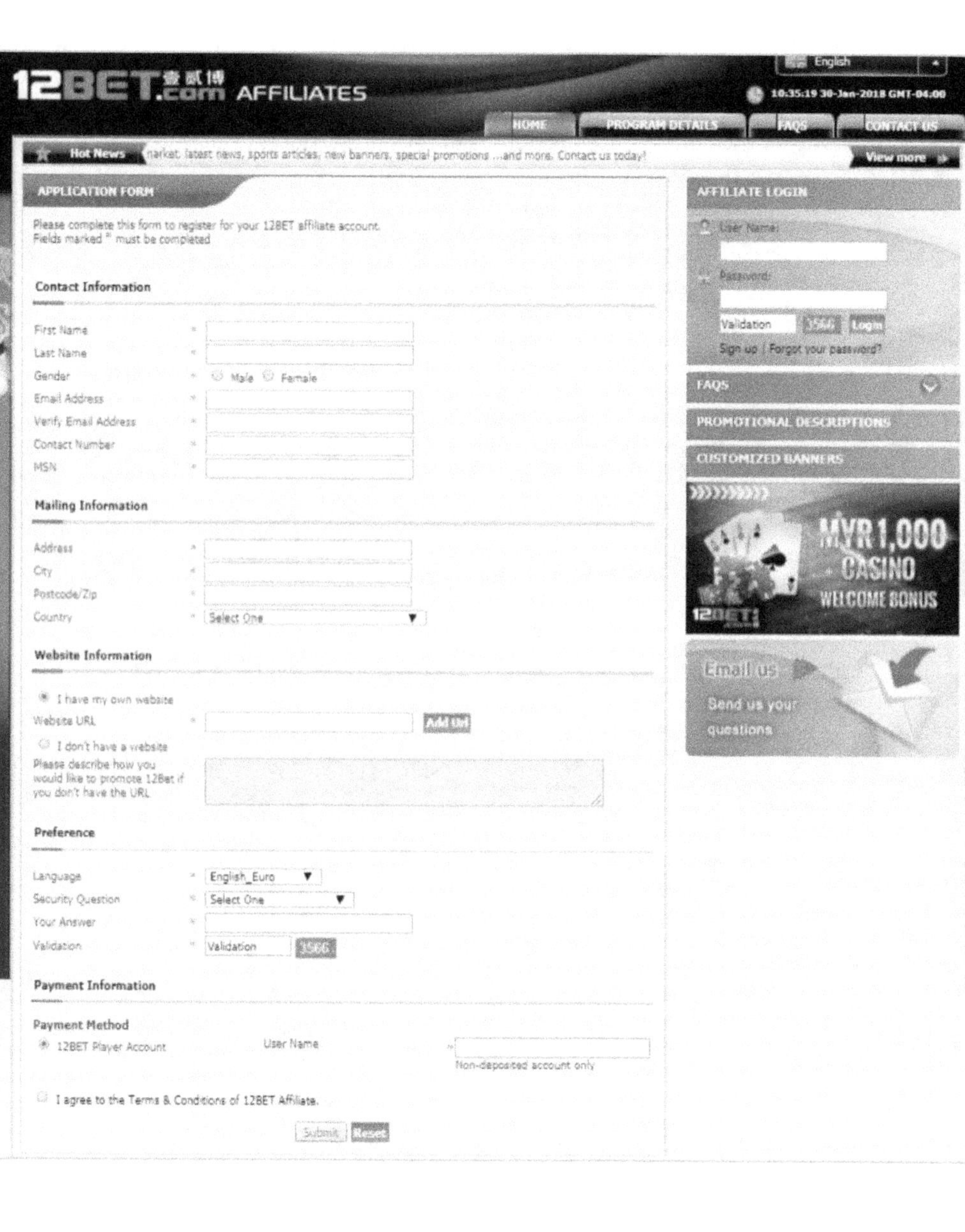

12BET.com 壹贰博 AFFILIATES

English

10:35:19 30-Jan-2018 GMT-04:00

HOME | PROGRAM DETAILS | FAQS | CONTACT US

Hot News — market, latest news, sports articles, new banners, special promotions ...and more. Contact us today! — View more

APPLICATION FORM

Please complete this form to register for your 12BET affiliate account.
Fields marked * must be completed

Contact Information

First Name *
Last Name *
Gender * Male Female
Email Address *
Verify Email Address *
Contact Number *
MSN *

Mailing Information

Address *
City *
Postcode/Zip *
Country * Select One

Website Information

I have my own website
Website URL * Add Url
I don't have a website
Please describe how you would like to promote 12Bet if you don't have the URL

Preference

Language * English_Euro
Security Question * Select One
Your Answer *
Validation * Validation 3566

Payment Information

Payment Method

12BET Player Account — User Name *
Non-deposited account only

I agree to the Terms & Conditions of 12BET Affiliate.

Submit Reset

AFFILIATE LOGIN

User Name:
Password:
Validation 3566 Login
Sign up | Forgot your password?

FAQS

PROMOTIONAL DESCRIPTIONS

CUSTOMIZED BANNERS

MYR1,000 CASINO WELCOME BONUS

Email us — Send us your questions

Revolut

Account Information

The technology for the Revolut affiliate program is provided by Impact. Please fill out this form to complete your application
If you already have an Impact account, please click the button below

Language: English (United Kingdom)

Company Name

Website: http://

Country / Region: United States

Bank Location Country: United States

Currency: USD US Dollar

Timezone: (GMT -08:00) Pacific Time (US & Canada)

It doesn't necessarily have to be on the same affiliate welcome page as mentioned above. This Terms and Conditions page can be within your existing user T&C's or within your own 'About us' section. It is good though to link to it from your welcome/sign up page.

These T&C's should outline the key terms of any third party site promoting you. It should describe how you will be accepted to the program, that you should use your brand according to the guidelines, it should in some part outline the commission structure, the payment procedure etc.

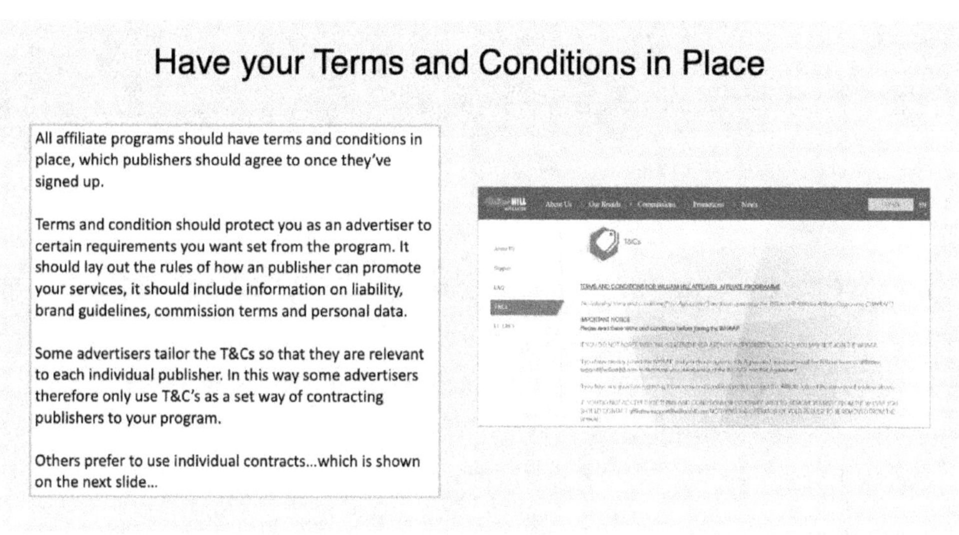

Alternatively, you could send them an affiliate agreement to sign. This does help officialise your program. And while you start off with 0–100 partners is a good idea. When you are much larger it might be easier for partners to accept T&C's onsite by simply ticking a box.

Or get them to sign your Affiliate Agreement

An essential part of the affiliate arrangement between publisher and advertiser is to agree terms via a contractual agreement. Signing an 'Affiliate Agreement' ensures both parties are clear what the terms of the publisher promoting the advertiser are into a legally binding contract.

Let's remind ourselves that this is the creation of a brand new channel within your business. And unless you've had a lot of interest to partner and promote your brand to date, it might be a case of advertising your program to recruit publishers.

We do come onto recruitment later on, but during the build phase you will need to create a sales deck.

Do not make your sales deck extremely long. Don't cover it in awards and explanations about how great your business is. Our recommendation is to make it about the publishers.

Explain from the start what is in it for them, how much they could earn, how easy it is to promote your products, and how well they convert over competitors. A handful of slides is fine, and now you have something to share with partners that perhaps might require a meeting or formal chat. Not all will require this, most will be happy to promote your brand aside from such information, but it's useful to have at hand in case they ask to understand more about your business.

As described above, you should have a brand guidelines document already at hand. Perhaps your design team have already produced one for general/internal use.

This document should explain how to use the brand colours, logos and tag lines in the correct way to 'stay on brand'.

With affiliate marketing it's vital that all publishers stick to your brand guidelines so that they describe, explain and important display you in the right way to their audience. There's nothing worse than 100's of third party sites all saying what they like about your products, all with a variation of your logo, and squashing and squeezing it in unusual ways. Keep everything on-brand and in sync with your other marketing channels.

Have your Brand Guidelines in place

Most advertisers due to copyright and trademark law are extremely protective about their brand. As shown in the contractual agreement this can be protected by outlining the terms of use. The Brand Guidelines document shows where and how the brand should be promoted, including logo design variations, colours and guidelines on tone of voice.

It is a document that the majority of brands produce and it is extremely supportive to a publisher to know how to promote an advertiser. Below is an example from the hugely recognisable global brand Skype that describes the recommended usage of their brand logo:

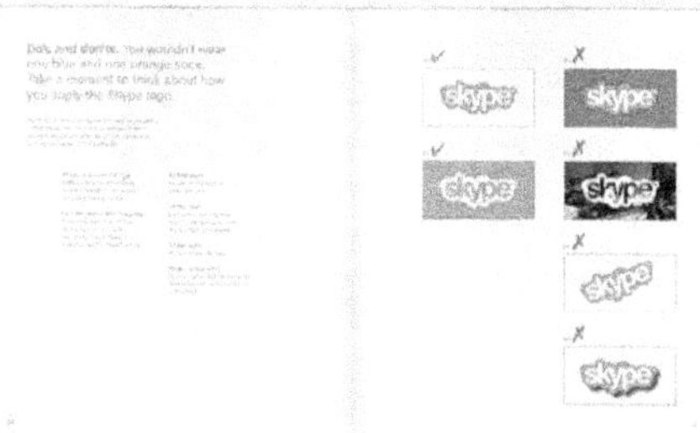

And lastly for the build phase, is to have FAQ's in place. This doesn't necessarily mean they have to be posted on-site, but they should be somewhere affiliates can read so that they understand more about what they are promoting and how the affiliate program works. Questions might be '*how often will I get paid?*', '*how do I find my tracking links?*', '*who do I contact if I have an issue?*' etc.

FAQ's are a great way to provide a really quick snapshot to both your existing and potentially new publishers. It covers off all the main points surrounding your program for them to understand without having to ask you a thing.

It should include questions like...

- How do I get approved to join your program?
- What commissions do you offer?
- What counts as a conversion? Etc.

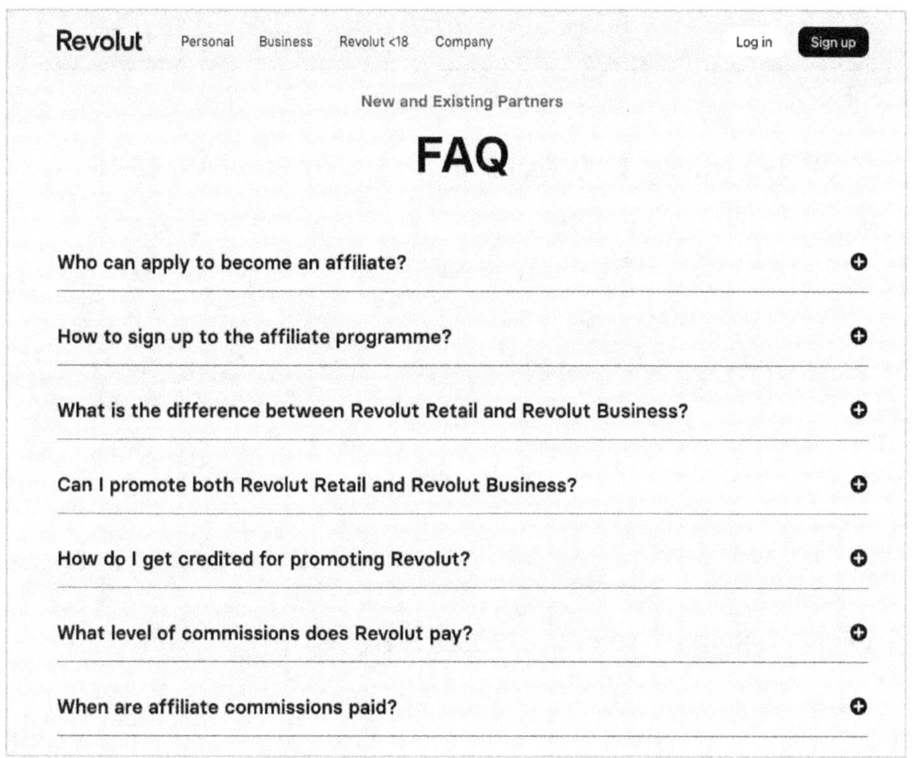

Step 3: Agencies & Networks

Step 3 to creating your affiliate and partnerships channel from scratch, is to make a decision on agencies and networks.

This very much joins with step 4, where we discuss recruitment and how to attract partners. Why we should consider agencies and networks prior to this, is to firstly understand what they offer and how they can benefit you. Not only to kick start your channel, but for the future too.

Below describes the differences between a network and an agency. In affiliate marketing particularly, networks play a huge role in attracting new publishers.

Networks can be public, like Awin's marketplace, where the advertisment of your affiliate program is public. While there also exists private networks, such as SaaS platforms like Partnerize or CAKE.

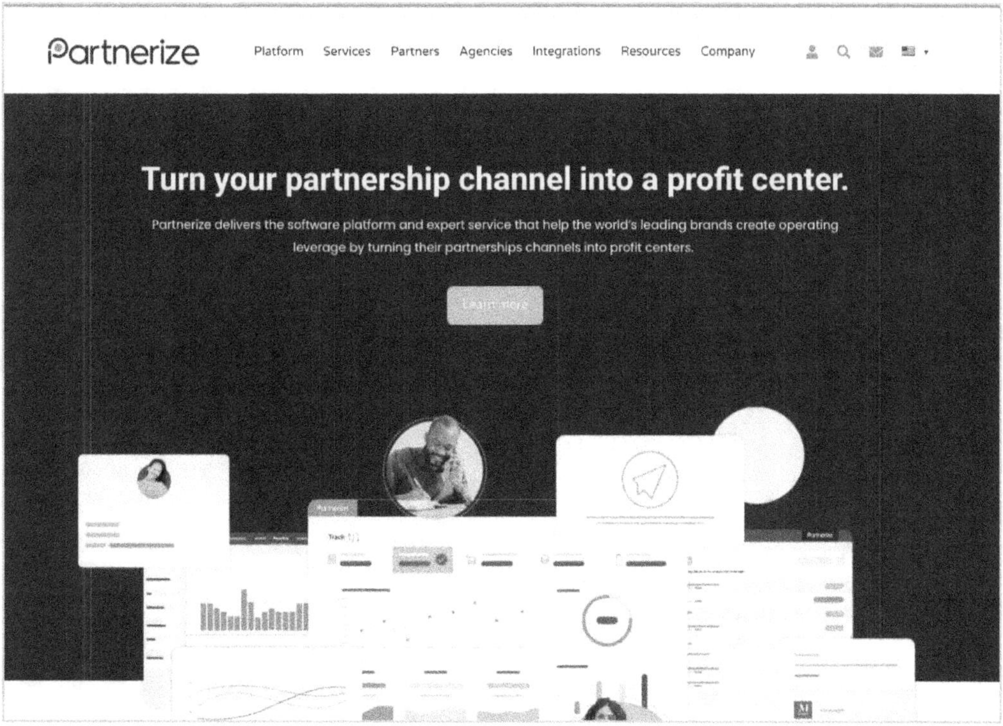

Partnerize

Platform Services Partners Agencies Integrations Resources Company

Turn your partnership channel into a profit center.

Partnerize delivers the software platform and expert service that help the world's leading brands create operating leverage by turning their partnerships channels into profit centers.

Agencies are a more expensive approach, as they take a cut of your commission or have an added override on top. But they very act as a right hand man when it comes to recruitment and channel strategy.

Lastly, going it alone certainly has it's advantages. It's cheaper for starters. Some partners often like a more hands on approach. You have more control and for partnership marketing, it means a more direct relationship, which often leads to improved results.

Decide whether to go it alone or join a Network

Once you have suitable internal tracking in place it's time to decide whether to reach out to publishers or whether to join a network and advertise your program there.

We've covered a lot about the benefits of an agency or network, but from initial stage the decision rests really on your type of product and industry. In the finance industry, as the publisher base is small, many advertisers feel they go it alone. In the gambling industry the publishers are vast, so it will simply be unmanageable alone.

- Network - join a network where you can upload your creatives and hey presto wait for publishers to grab them and start promoting your services.
- Go it alone - with an in-house solution like Google Analytics, or a tech tool like CAKE and manage your affiliates with a hands-on approach.
- Agency - a quick but more expensive option is to work with an agency. The advantages here are they recruit affiliates on your behalf and manage the admin.

Before we move on to step 4 and actually talk about recruitment, lets delve a bit deeper into what networks and agencies can offer.

Firstly, networks offer a two sided marketplace and ready-made portal to host your affiliate assets, such as creatives, T&C's, commission breakdowns, performance reports and much more.

Utilising a Network

What is a Network?

- Think of a network as a marketplace for affiliate publishers and advertisers.
- They advertise publishers to advertisers, while also advertising advertiser affiliate programs to publishers, so they can promote their products or services.
- The network allows both parties to login and see their stats.
- From a client-side / advertiser perspective it's a great way to advertise your affiliate program, attract new publishers and analyse all your affiliate results with one login, in one place

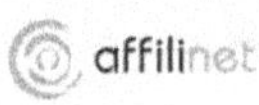

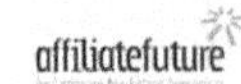

Networks do come in all shapes and sizes, but they're there to be a one-stop shop for all your affiliate and partnership channel needs. Think of it as an out-of-the-box solution to start and run your channel. Often very much a go-to starting point for many channels.

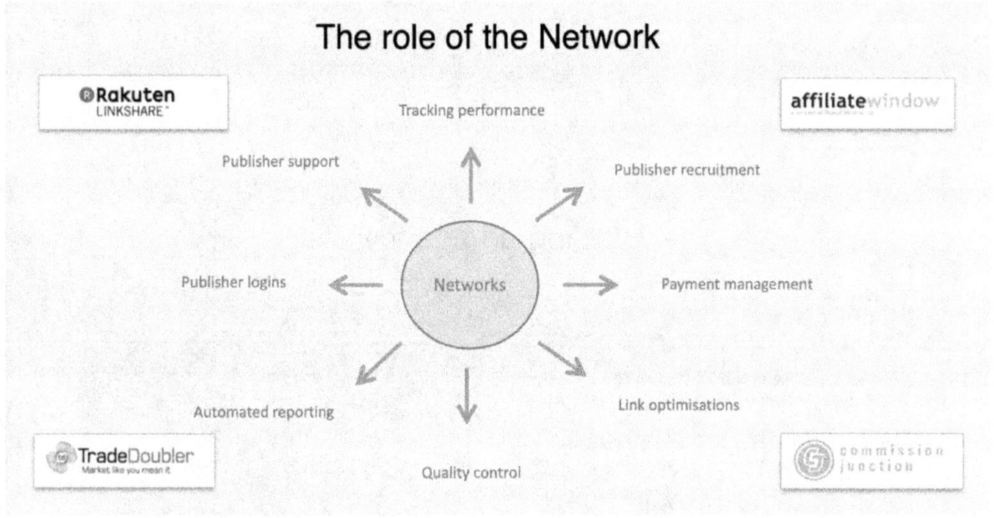

Secondly, agencies act slightly differently to networks. Although some may have a marketplace of their own, where you can locate publishers, agencies often host account managers and strategists to help start and grow your channel. Think of it as having another dedicated affiliate manager who has the connections and can introduce you to publishers or partners extremely easily. For rapid growth, this is a common go-to for some brands.

Utilising an agency

What is an agency?

- Lets firstly mention that a network can also be an agency.
- Some networks, like Awin and OMG also offer an agency service to their advertiser community.
- With this they tend to sell their account management and strategic skills to help grow your affiliate program.
- Agencies will charge a commission for this, what they call an override.
- Depending on the complexity of your affiliate program an agency can be highly valuable to an advertiser.
- A lot of what we cover in the strategic section will include the assistance of an agency. Whether it be from a fully-fledged strategic plan to simply negotiating placements or recruiting new affiliates on your behalf.

Agencies help to guide you on your strategic direction. They introduce you to better tracking technology, they analyse the market, manage your reporting and help with recruitment. This does though come at a cost, so is it right for your channel when it's just starting off?

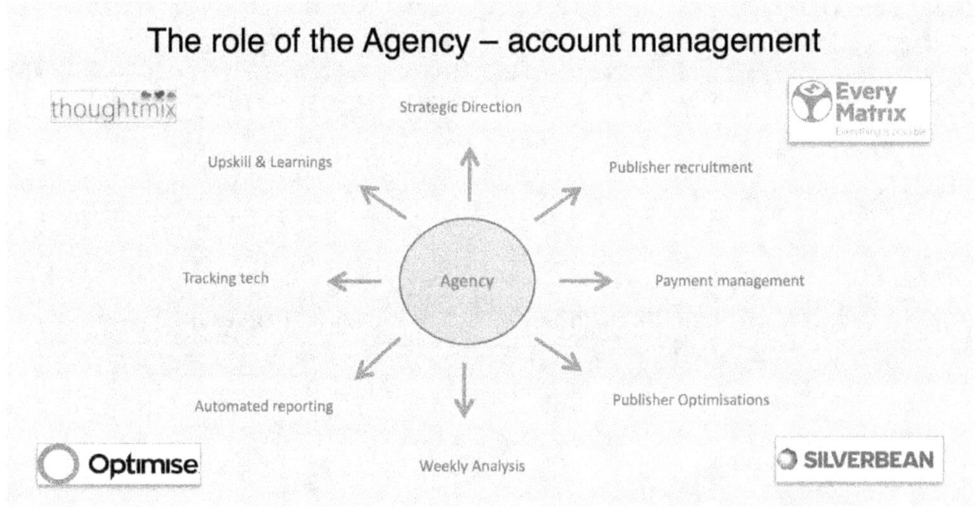

Step 4: Recruitment

Moving on now to one of the most important elements of this guide — recruitment.

Before you even have your first publisher or partner our exclusive technique, is to create a Recruitment Map.

Imagine being able to have full oversight, a complete picture, of the industry you are in and who would be available to partner with. That's what the Recruitment

Map is aiming to do. With this picture you can then breakdown who to work with and reach out to them.

As described below, this simple exercise is just a case of writing down each and every brand you're aware of and categorising them. Whether you believe they are out of reach, whether they are a publisher or advertiser, whether they aren't even in your industry necessarily — it's a case of splitting them into a visual map.

Build out your map by using your own knowledge, your colleagues and online and offline research. Why not also write down a contact's contact details beside each partner name. Maybe even colour code them for most likely to work with you to least likely. This invaluable exercise will give you an excellent starting point on your recruitment journey.

How to recruit affiliates - The Recruitment Map

- The idea is essentially a mind-map; jot down and categorise every relevant brand and site you can think of that will resonate with your customers.
- As an example, in the finance industry I immediately think of the big three; Moneysupermarket, Money.co.uk and Moneysavingexpert.
- The sites listed here will range from tiny cookery blogs that just your mum reads, to huge cashback sites such as Topcashback or Quidco.
- A tip is to refine the map by highlighting the ones you are sure your customers use, with the largest reach, and those you already have a connection with.

Once you've established who to target there are plenty of ideas how to attract and recruit them. Rather than going into too much detail here, we've compiled the top 50 ways of finding new partners in our latest book...

'How to find new Affiliates and Partners; With over 50+ ideas for Affiliate Managers!'

This slide below also highlights some of the ideas whether you're going it alone, or utilising a network or agency...

How to recruit affiliates – advertise your program

Going Alone

- So you currently have no publishers...as mentioned, first stage is to create an affiliate recruitment map so you know who to reach out to...
- Create an affiliate page on your site to organically attract requests from publishers.
- Take this one step further have a program they can literally sign up to and login there and then.
- Create a deck to advertise the key elements of your program and start distributing these to known contacts.
- Scour the internet for websites where your competitors are placed. Utilise Google search and social media.
- If you have no competitors in your space who are active in affiliation, then get researching into what sites you think would promote your products/services.
- Start asking around internally and gather a list of contacts and add these to your affiliate map to reach out to.
- Go to industry events – if you have a big budget higher a booth.

Network or Agency

- We will come onto Agencies...but they can be a useful asset to reach out to potential publishers. They will reach out on your behalf but cost you an override of about 20% per new customer.
- An agency that's also a network will do the same thing but have a base which will be visible to you to reach out to.
- A network without the agency element simply gives you access to the range of publishers on that network...
- For this you should make sure your profile on that network is as attractive as can be.
- Offer a competitive commission rate and have your creative ready and waiting for publishers to pick it up
- Arrange a referral program for some of your affiliates you've just acquired so you can get more. Offer them a cut back if they refer others.

After a recruitment drive, utilising the ideas mentioned above, you might become inundated with requests. Now we do come on to explain which partners are right for you in more detail in step 5, and the difference between partner sizes. But its important to review and approve which affiliates and partners you want to work with.

Reviewing and Approving Affiliates to join your program

Once you've set in place your affiliate recruitment tactics, including advertising for new publishers across your network, they will start to come to you requesting to join. An important part of growth stages is to understand which publishers are right for you and those that are not and approving accordingly. My top tips for reviewing and approving are:

- Finding out the site's monthly active users and traffic
- Sites with poor track record of incorrect voucher codes, abuse, treating their users poorly, not giving the cashback timely.
- Any site which doesn't relate to your product - remember you want to the right customers, not just any customer!

How do I get my site approved?

1. Please make sure to follow the Marketing Rules, while inserting content. The full Marketing Rules list is available on your affiliate account, after log in.
2. Choose from our variety of marketing tools (banners, widgets, articles etc.) available in your affiliate account and implement them on your website.
3. Submit your website for our review in your affiliate account https://www.500affiliates.com/Account/Reports/ApprovedURLs.aspx
4. Once your site is approved you can refer traffic to Plus500 from it.

How to pay partners is an important consideration at this stage. Before stage 5, where you will begin to grow your channel, and we take you on each phase of that growth journey, you should decide on your commission model. Knowing what you are able to pay a partner is vitally important.

You should look at competitor rates, determine your margin per sale and how much commission per sale you can pass on to the affiliate. Depending on your product, will you be offering a share of revenue, or a one off commission for each sale. Perhaps paying on sale is not the right model.

For example car manufactures, such as BMW or Ford, won't pay their affiliates on per car sold, as it's a rare occurrence, instead they might pay per click.

This is a key area because it will determine what affiliates you can attract, how competitive your channel will be, and it'll impact your bottom line profit margins.

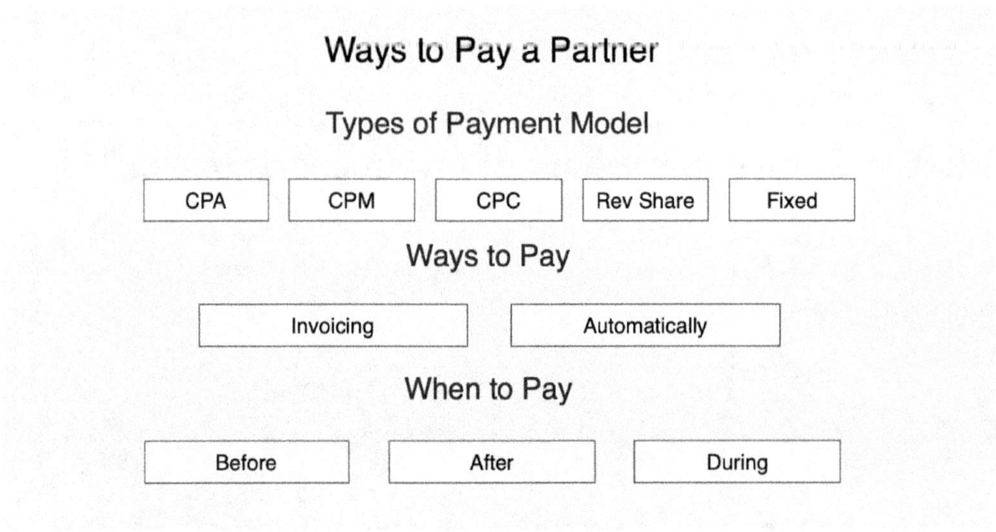

Ways to Pay a Partner

Types of Payment Model

CPA | CPM | CPC | Rev Share | Fixed

Ways to Pay

Invoicing | Automatically

When to Pay

Before | After | During

As mentioned above, there are various ways to pay out partners. Here they are explained. Most opt for CPA or Revenue Share, but it may depend on the product you are selling, the preference of the affiliate, or the package deal you are arranging with them. There's no right or wrong answer here, but you want a type that works for your business.

Commission Types & Negotiating Rates

- CPA – most advertisers offer their publishers a cost per acquisition. This is a one off payment for each sale. For advertisers this is preferred as it's a simple method where they can estimate easily how much it'll be costing them per month. For a publisher though they might push towards a revenue share or fixed cost where they could essentially earn more.
- Revenue share – providing commission as a percentage of each sale. Advertisers where the value of customers have a large range would most likely offer a share of their revenue. This might make more sense as they have both low and high value customers and want to attract the full range. The downside is that it's harder to estimate each month as it depends on which range of customer comes in.
- Fixed costs – some publishers push for a fixed cost or tenancy payment. This benefits the publisher as they are guaranteed payment. And for the advertiser it also ensures what they will spend. But if the returns don't equal the fixed payment then it's not efficient.
- Hybrid – other publishers can be more complex in their requests. Some will demand a complicated structure of CPA and revenue share, in order protect themselves and earn more.
- Other – there is also CPC, CPM and CPL.
- Tiered – lets also mention a tiered structure, which many advertisers prefer as it rewards publishers for bringing in more.

Step 5: Growth

Now onto the growth step, where we'll be looking ways you can develop your affiliate and partner channel from small to large.

It's important to say at this stage number-of-affiliates is not the key indicator of growth. This metric will depend on your size as a company as well as size of the industry you're in. It's not say that if you reach a ceiling of 50 affiliates you have failed, rather it should be a dependant a number of factors.

Such as, the size of the channel compared to other marketing channels, the revenue it brings in, the quality of customer it acquires, the level of branding exposure it achieves, or any other marketing metric you may be ultimately judging it upon.

For this exercise though lets look at number of affiliates and how to expand that number and the quality of affiliates in unison.

From 10–50:

Before we even jump in we need to know what a healthy affiliate program looks like.

A typical affiliate channel has a combination of super, headline, medium and long tail affiliates. The slide below describes these, and the aim of an affiliate manager is to get a nice healthy mix of each type.

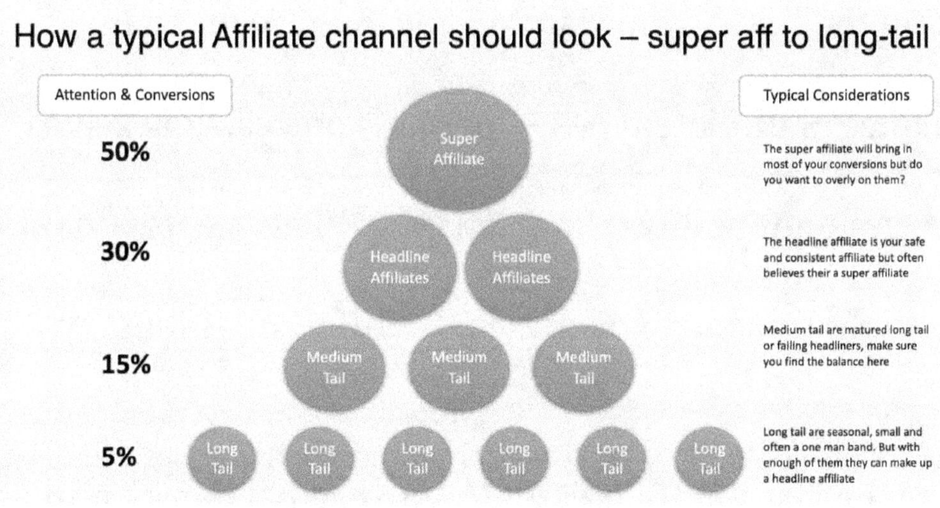

If super affiliates make up 80% of your revenue (even if they are 10% of your number-of-affiliates) is this a healthy balance? You are in fact over-relying on them. So the aim should be to recruit a nice blend of all types to balance out revenue.

The above chapters cover how to start your channel, and we did previously discuss how to recruit your first 5 affiliates.

From the first 5, you want to start aiming for again a balance of affiliate types – perhaps one cashback site, two content, and two long tail blogs. This starts you on the right track to expanding into different affiliate types.

Like the size of affiliates slide above, a balance of affiliate type is also crucial, so you don't over-rely on cashback. What if the CEO turns round one day and says I don't want us doing cashback anymore? Your affiliate channel falls flat on it's feet.

With the first 5 let them have some exclusive content. To get them started, why not write the content for them to simply upload. Make their life as easy as possible to promote you. As little work as a publisher or partner needs to do to send traffic to you the better.

They're also more likely to promote you, an affiliate manager who makes saves them time, than a competitor who expects them to do all the work.

Start building a close bond and friendship with the first few affiliates. They should be your most loyal partners as time goes by.

Create co-branded pages for them, and push for top placements across their site. If they have a comparison table, what is it they need for your brand to feature at the very top? And can you match their requirements.

Why not give them an exclusive promotional offer or discount, give them favourable commission rates – what we're saying is, treat them like VIP's as you need these partners to really kick off your channel.

Later on you will see, it's much easier to recruit when you have more case studies and name-drops!

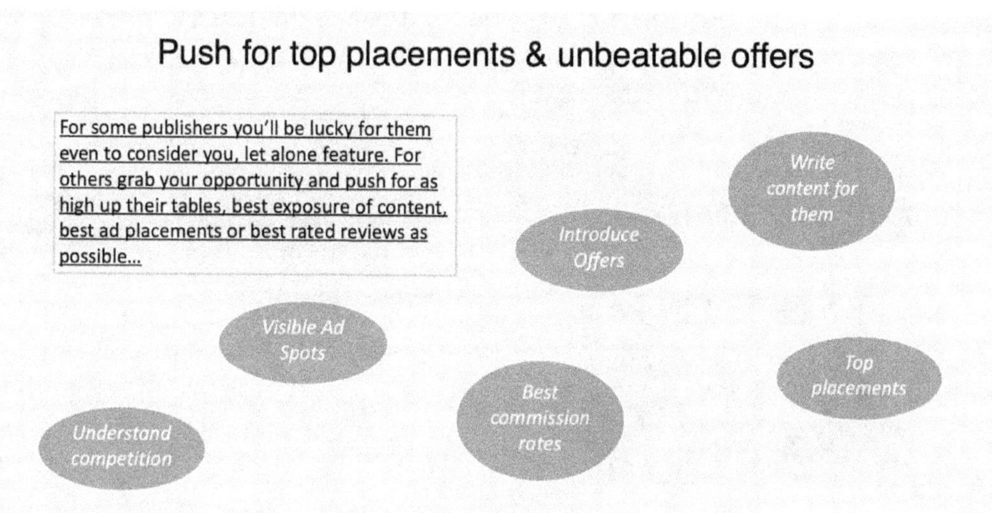

As mentioned, co-branded pages work a treat. This is because it connects the customer from one site to the next and the publisher site loves the idea of their brand being on your site. It also helps conversion too in many cases, again that brand association playing a key part. Offer this to your first few partners.

Encourage Co-branded Landing Pages

Co-branded landing pages typically have higher conversion than non-co-branded. Publishers love the idea of having a co-branded page, so introduce a template splash page where the logo of a publisher can easily be switched out for another – this way replicating co-branded pages easily...

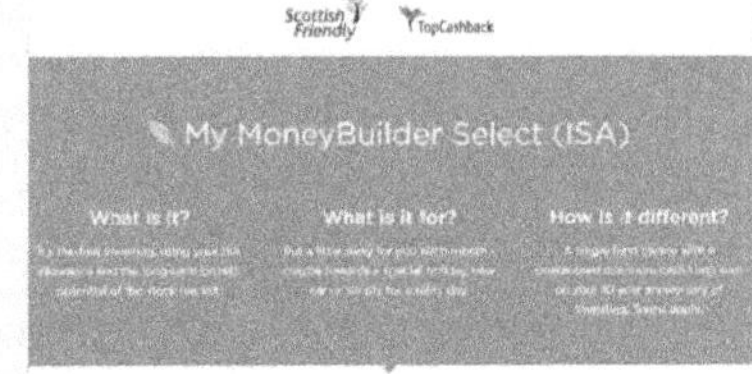

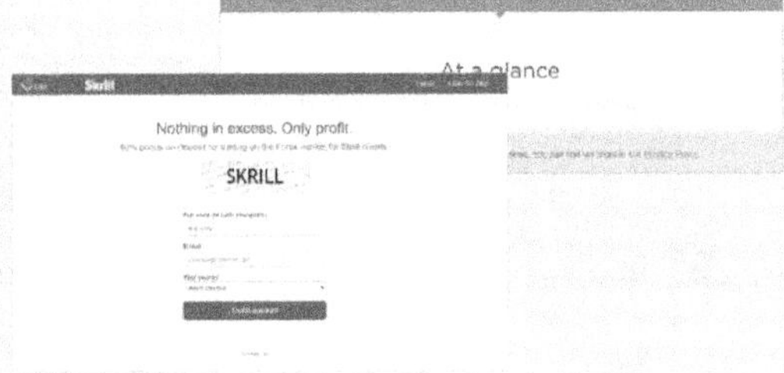

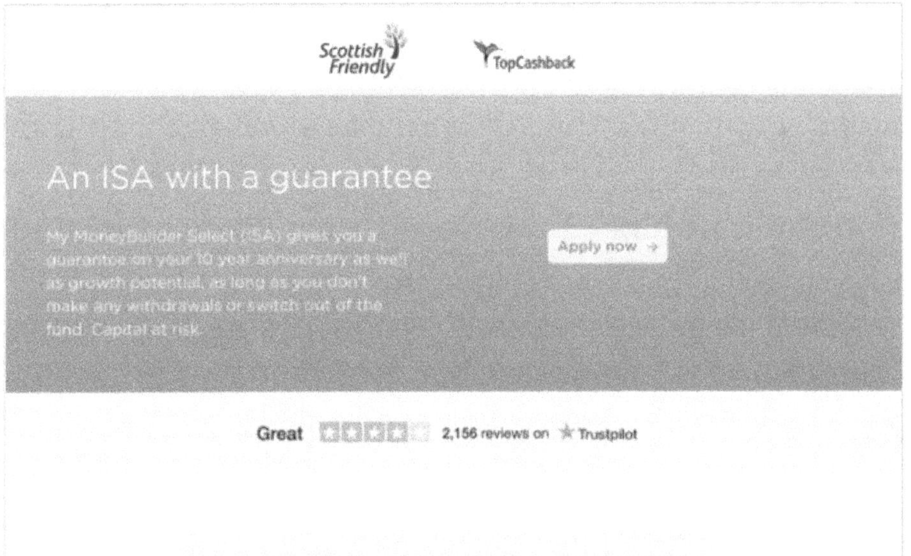

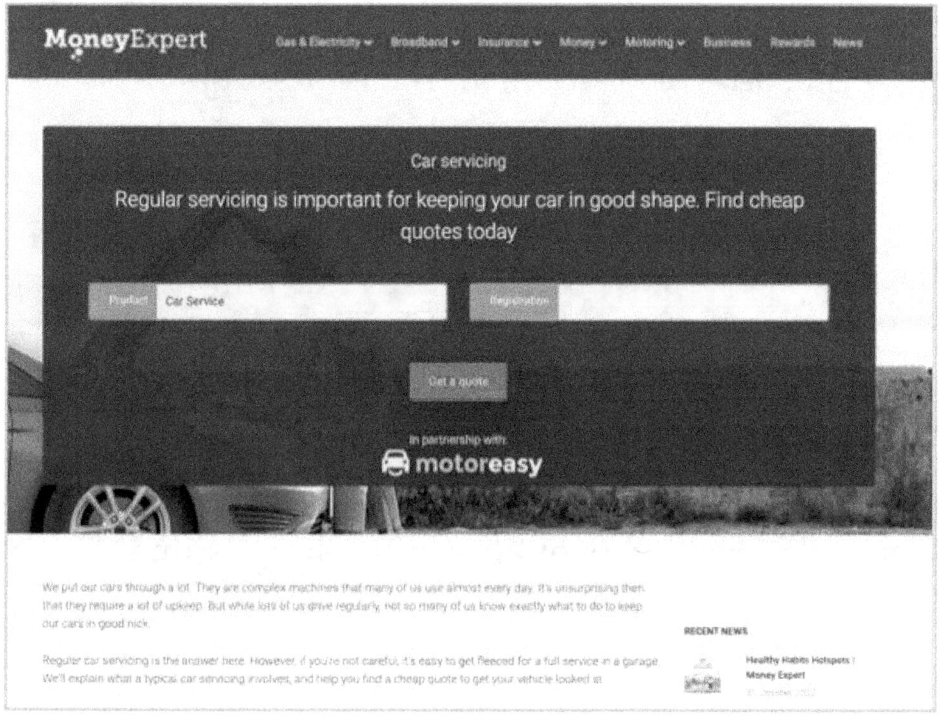

From 50–100:

Great, you have your first few partners, lets now use this as a spring-board to get to 50–100. Right now you have a small, workable base to work from. You should analyse and utilise them to grow.

Analyse your first 10 or so partners and notice which are converting and/or bringing in the highest quality customers. Perhaps it's voucher code sites that are working very well for you. It's with this knowledge that you should start to go and recruit more of them.

Secondly, focus on hospitality and relationships. Continue to establish a long-term working relationship with your first 10–20 partners. Try and lock them in to long-term agreements too if you can.

If you're using a network, start analysing the partner requests that come in and pick ones that might suit your channel. Why not also introduce a 'refer a friend' affiliate scheme, where existing partners can benefit from referring new ones — therefore organically growing your channel.

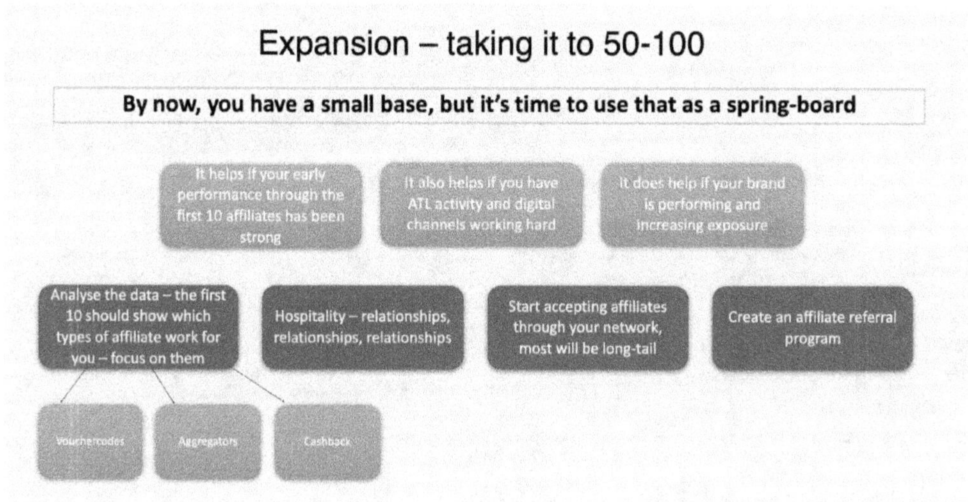

If you've employed most of the recruitment techniques we've previously mentioned you should start to develop a recruitment funnel.

The illustration below shows what a recruitment funnel could visually look like. This gives all affiliate channel stakeholders a clear idea of who you're speaking to and who might join. If your list is extensive this can be adapted to excel, listing out each phase of your recruitment process and where the conversations are at.

Keep working on relationship building, even if the number of publishers and partners is growing to a high number of 50–100. It should still be manageable enough for you to meet, invite and gift — even if just with your important partners.

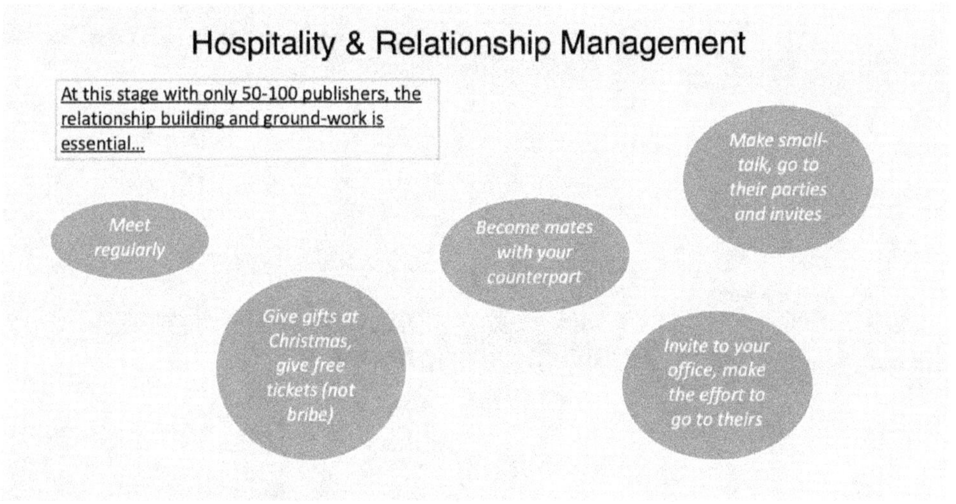

Lastly, analysis is key at this stage. You really want to learn which partners are working for you. Which affiliate type is performing the best and try to understand why this is and if it can be replicated.

Don't be concerned at this stage if many of your partners are not converting yet. This is a growing channel at this stage and you may find only 30% of those recruited are bringing in customers. This just means the other 70% are long-tail. What's important is the blend of partners and the weighting of revenue (remember our super affiliates vs long-tail slide).

Analysing Performance

		Agency	Jan-19	Feb-19	Mar-19
Cashback	Quidco	Awin	278	219	516
	TopCashBack	Awin	217	118	861
	ExtraCash	Awin			
	Earncashback	Awin			116
Voucher	MyVoucherCodes	Awin			
	Promocodes	Direct		2	
	Comparethis	Direct			21
	Discounts.com	Awin			
Aggregator	Moneysupermarket	Direct	15	6	15
	Money.co.uk	Direct	112	8	17
	Moneywise	Direct			1
	MoneySuperstore	Direct			
	Moneyfactuals	Direct	4	3	2
	Off3r	Direct			
	Wealthcompare	Direct			
	Fairlyinvesting	Direct			
	Isa.co.uk	Direct			4
Content	MoneysavingExpert	Direct	912	1119	3110
	Moneytothemasses	Direct	1	5	8
	Instagram Influencers	Direct			43
	Lovemoney	Direct		2	21
	Thisismoney	Direct		2	11
	Dailymail	Direct	5	2	
	TheMirror	Direct			
	Financial Times	Direct			11
	Prosperify	Direct			
	GoodBrokerGuide	Direct		3	

10%
20%
50%
20%

20%
25%
15%
40%

From 100–1000:

Great news, you're up to 100 affiliates. This is where some channels may stop, not because they fail but because the industry opportunity is not large enough. It may also not make sense to go beyond 100.

If only 25 of your 100 are converting, would it make sense to keep recruiting long-tail partners that offer nothing. This is a judgement call and it depends on the number of partners currently converting with you and if there is opportunity for more.

Start looking at a broader picture with your program now. Look at motivation techniques for partners, like commission structures, competitions, and account management attention provided.

It might also be time to look at sub-affiliation, using a CRM system to reach out to them all, and utilising an agency. These more advanced areas are all part of a larger affiliate program.

The reason for activities like a CRM system, is that when you approach 200–500 and then up to 1000 partners it can't be managed on a one-on-one basis. This should be reserved for the super partners.

Instead you'll need to start treating your affiliates like customers, and communicating with them on mass and running competitions etc to encourage them to refer more.

Expansion -100 to1000 Publishers

You now have a fully fledged affiliate channel which should be contributing to your business growth. For some advertisers 100 publishers might be all they can achieve, it depends on the industry size. For others it's time to take it to 1,000...

We should note, it's not actually about the size of your publisher base that makes your channel successful, so many of these initiatives should be implemented if you remain at 100 publishers or less...

80-20 rule – focus on the top 20 that bring in 80% of the results

Continue to expand your long-tail – your long-tail is worth 2 super affiliates

Motivate, Network, Account Manage, Pay on time, adapt commissions

Sub-affiliates, email comms, larger advertiser team, promotions

Despite what we may have been saying, if there is any point in recruiting more and more long-tail. The real question is do they convert?

If they literally never do convert then you need to question if the branding exposure you receive on their sites is still worth it — it may be, and they might even be assisting conversions (you'll need to look at your attribution for this and if they are contributing you may wish to award them accordingly). But some channels may find they do convert rarely, but often enough that it can add up if you have enough of them.

Say for example in the finance industry, some channels may find huge spikes in activity around the end of the financial tax year (which is the beginning of April in the

U.K.). This might result in some long-tail partners converting who haven't sent you a single customer all year. Then consider this — what if you had hundreds of them? Then they will add up!

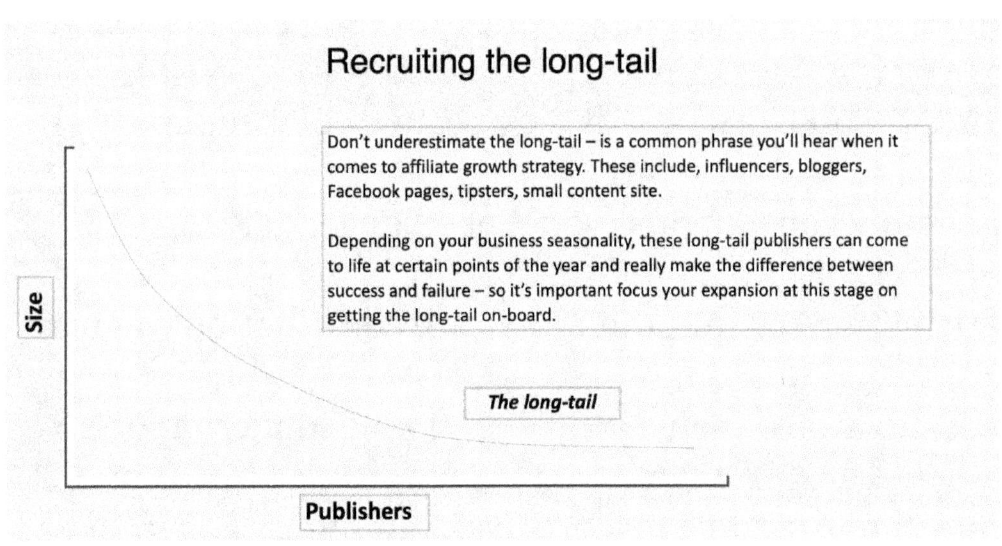

At this stage it's important to consider what role exclusivity plays. You might be giving special offers to some partners — perhaps your top affiliates have demanded it. It certainly helps conversion. But does is it at the determent of other partners, meaning all top partners with the special offer steal the conversion, and the other partners miss out? Don't forget customers browse many sites across the net before buying!

Exclusivity

Exclusive Offers mean that the customer cannot get this offer anywhere else. Most advertisers are willing to offer publishers exclusive offers but only if performance is at an acceptable level or the demand is there. To expand your base to 100+ introducing exclusive offers and using them to onboard or motivate publishers is one of the main tools you have at your disposal.

If you're going to offer an exclusive offer or promotion to a publisher make sure you negotiate accordingly. You want the top placement for this exclusivity or you want them to refer you another publisher before offering it out.

Also remember, the more you dish out, the less impact they have. They are no longer exclusive – so pick your publishers wisely.

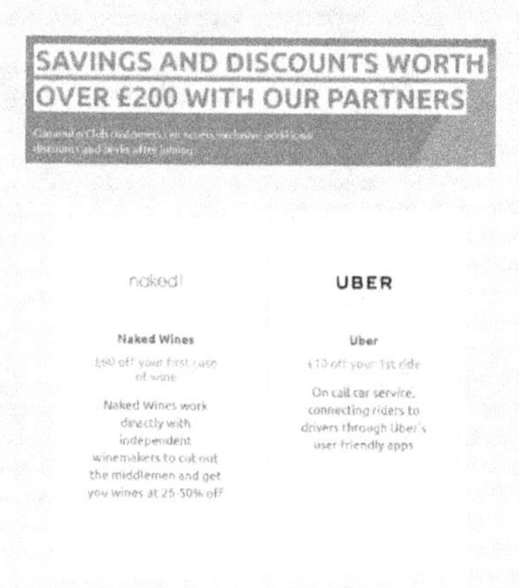

As mentioned, promotions and competitions are a great way to motivate your partners. If you have enough of them then why not create get them to compete against each other for extra commissions. You will benefit massively from the extra exposure it'll bring.

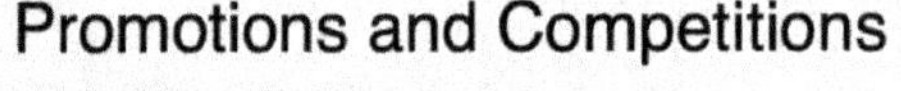

Promotions and competitions are a great way to motivate your publishers – there's more on this in the next section. There are both promotions to your customers via publishers – these come in the form of exclusive offers. There are also competitions direct to publishers to encourage them to recruit for you or convert at a higher rate.

Customer Offers & Competitions

- Monetary discount
- Percentage discount
- Buy-one get one-free
- Additional Prize, Gift or Toy
- Loyalty Club members
- Specific Customer Segment Only
- Limited Time Only
- Geographic Location Only
- Volume Usage Only
- Integrated services

Publisher Competitions

- Most converted
- Time-limited
- League table
- Highest value
- Most referred publishers
- Group competitions
- 5-a-side meet ups

Some more motivation techniques now. And this is the stage to employ them. You have enough partners where areas such as tiered commission structures and hospitality start to make a difference.

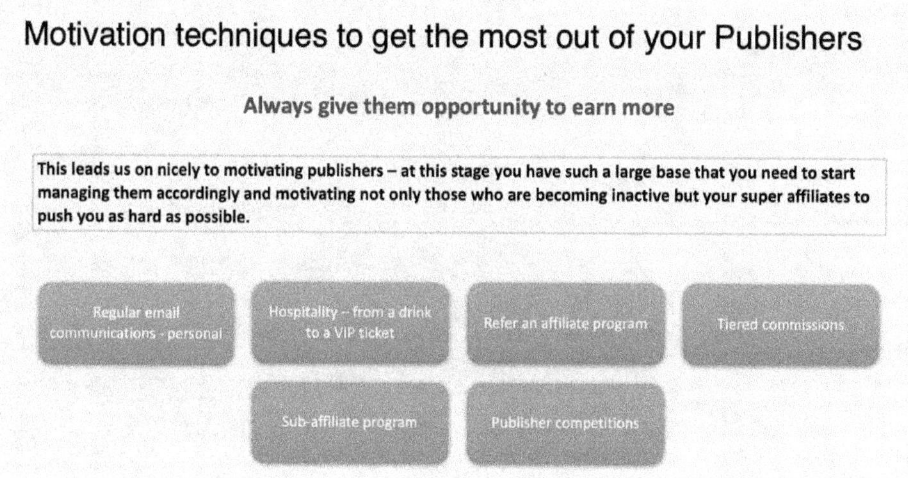

We discussed long-tail partners above, but lets not distract ourselves, super-affiliates are the ones that bring the true success. They will bring the revenue and quality customers, so put a bulk of your efforts into these.

It's balancing act of high attention while always trying to recruit more super partners. There is though often a finite number of these — huge commercial sites in your country don't come in abundance.

Getting the most out of your super affiliates

Remember the 80-20 rules – put 80% of your effort into these

Super affiliates are your top performing affiliates – treat them like they deserve and you'll reap the rewards. Tip's to improve the super elite...

Lastly for 100–1000 partners, we've outlined what you should do for each publisher type and how to get the most out of them. They are all different and have their own different qualities, so varying techniques will be needed to get the manage them...

- **Aggregators** - Push for the highest in the table, stand out with special offers / discounts, make sure your description is as strong and clear as it can be.

- **Content** - Provide the content for them, encourage favourable reviews.
- **Email** - Understand the data, test headlines, introduce special offers.
- **Bloggers** - As many as possible, often considered long-tail, make sure to keep an eye on them and regulate.
- **Influencers** - Monitor closely, use platforms, track accordingly, some might be better off as a branded campaign than acquisition.
- **Cashback** - Test tenancies and optimise until you have the most favourable packages, vary the rates between seasons and sites, monitor

the value that comes through - are customers of good quality.

- **Voucher** - Utilise codes, track accordingly, monitor any voucher abuse.

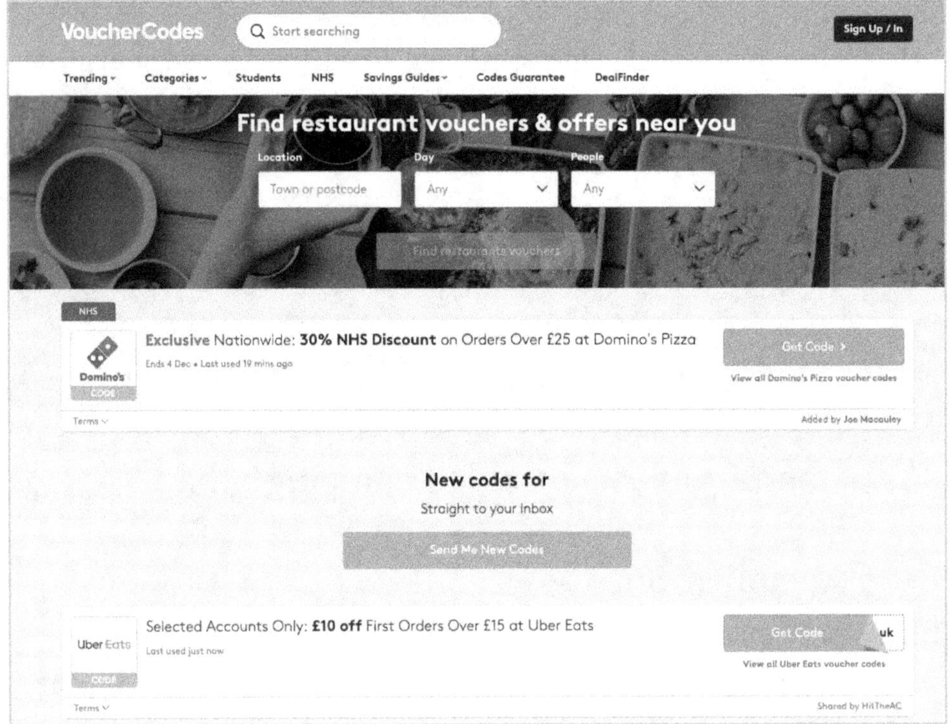

Over 1000:

In some industries and for some large brands, they may find the number of partners expand to 1000+. Again, size doesn't always equal success, but certainly if you've reached this number then you've done something right.

Channels of this size often need whole teams dedicated to managing it. This is why we set aside 'agencies and networks' as a chapter above. Because here you may very well be utilising them heavily.

For an affiliate channel of this magnitude you will need a team. Maybe not one as large as this, but it certainly helps to have a mix of '*Head of*' to oversee strategy, '*Affiliate Manager*' to a recruiter and account manager, as well as '*Executive*', a more junior member to assist. An analyst too might also be useful to help with performance reporting.

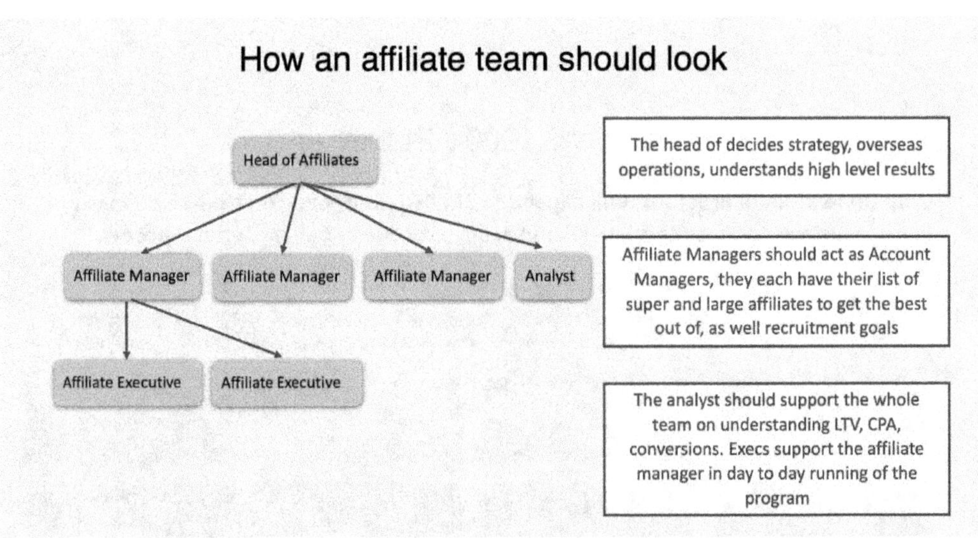

At this stage your program may well be self-serve. It is something we do recommend. This is because long-tail partners are clearly converting for you, so you should have dedicated area where they can sign up, grab creatives and start promoting you, without too much intervention from yourselves as channel owner. Imagine handling thousands of partners one on one, a self-serve option is one of the best routes here.

Right tech, right support, self-serve and dynamic ads

Dynamic ads -

- To be advanced in your affiliate marketing ads should be dynamic, meaning publishers can upload them to their sites but the messaging is controlled on your end.

- Lets say you want to show a specific message at the weekend such as an offer or relevant text, this allows you to have control and change it without having to ask the publisher to amend it on their end everytime.

Self-serve -

- Your platform should be fully self-serve. With this many publishers it's almost impossible to manage them all individually. So many will be able to self-select and your affiliate managers are there essentially for support.

- Self-serve means they can grab their own tracking links, banners and reports.

Right support -

- As shown, your affiliate managers should also be account managers. By that we mean that they should look after 2-3 super affiliates, 5-10 large and several hundred long-tail.
- This way they can dedicate their time accordingly and know who they need to be on hand to support.
- Support should be considered as tracking, payments, logins etc.

As our previous chapter covered, let agencies do a lot of the hard work if you can. Push them to recruit and incentivise them with the right commission structure to strategies, report and ultimately be your right-hand-man in your affiliate mission.

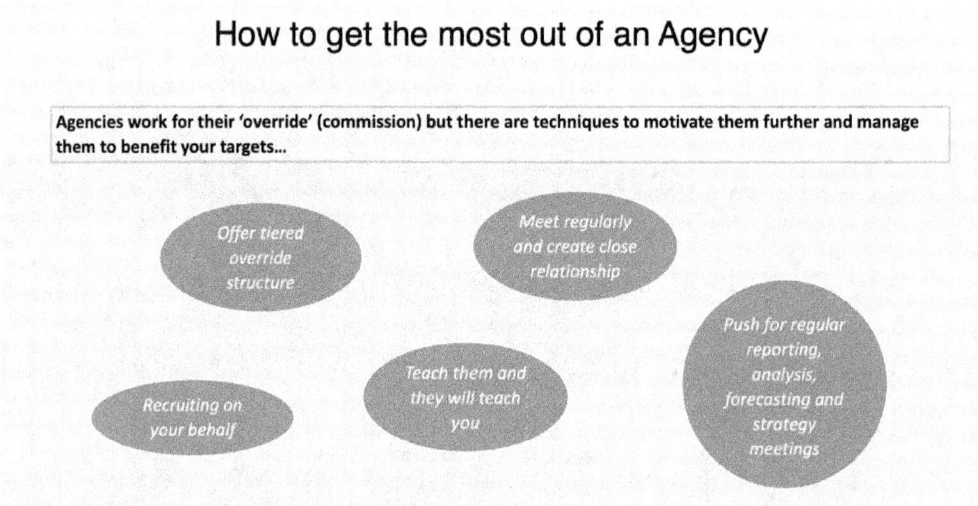

Your time should be focused on the bigger picture, as a complete channel. It's areas like landing page optimisation that can have a large overall impact. A-B test your different landing pages on segments of affiliates to see if they effect conversion.

Tests like this where you can utilise groups of partners and them deploy it across all, are where your strategic mind should be.

Continue to very much work across the data. At this stage you have so many publishers that the data will inform you what is or what isn't successful.

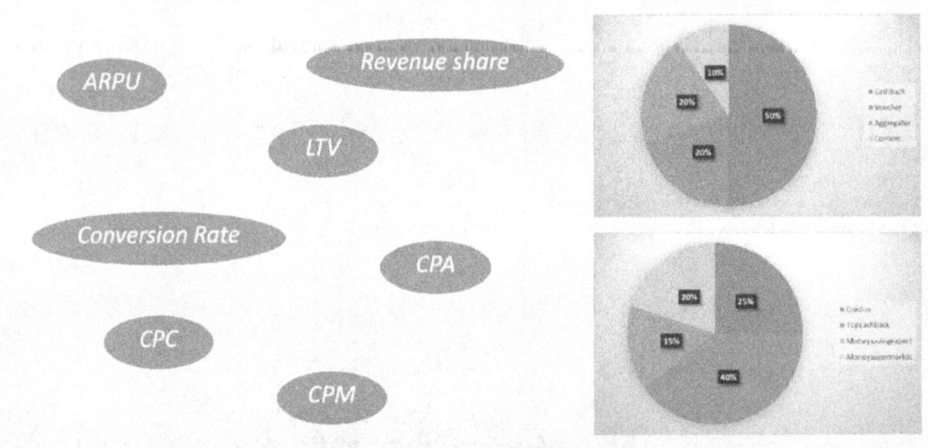

It won't all be rosy as your affiliate program grows, and at this level like all others, you will experience churn — partners dropping out. With this you should always try to keep them if they are an effective partner. Understand why they don't wish to promote you anymore and see what will turn it around — more commission perhaps?

Try to reactivate old partners too. Offer them a new product of yours to promote, better commission, inform them of your new branding and how well their competitors are doing at promoting you.

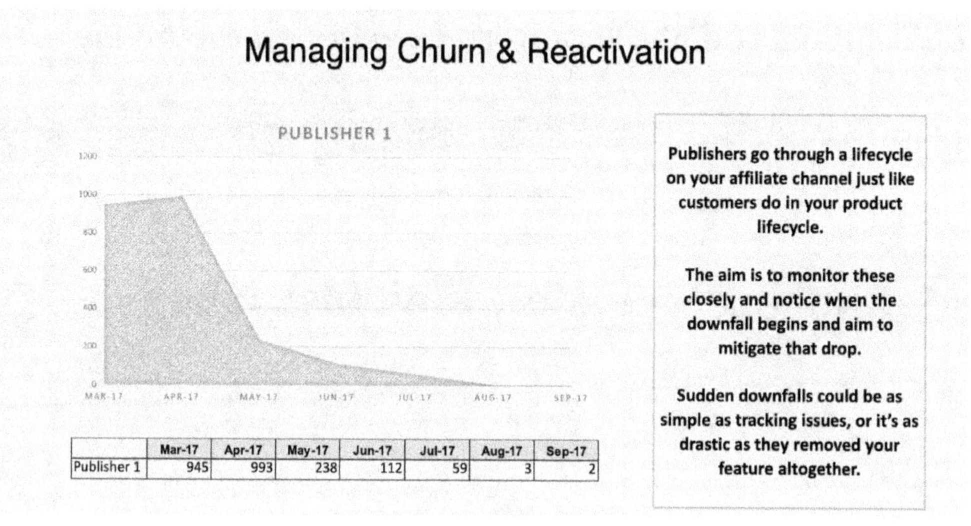

	Mar-17	Apr-17	May-17	Jun-17	Jul-17	Aug-17	Sep-17
Publisher 1	945	993	238	112	59	3	2

And lastly, a key area for any affiliate manager at this scale, is to monitor and don't lose touch. Keeping on top of how you are promoted is key.

Don't let partners go rogue or promote you without any policing. You don't want lies about your brand across multiple sites, you don't want your branding mis-placed.

It's important to essentially regulate your many partners at scale. It should be noted there are many platforms that can help with this, such as Partnerize who offer a dedicated fraud and monitoring section of their Saas platform.

Monitoring on scale - don't lose touch

Tipsters -

- In my experience in the gaming industry, and through many reports - tipsters, who made up most of their long-tail publishers were making up odds, writing what they wanted, and losing a lot of followers money - misleading them.
- All because the advertiser wasn't monitoring them closely enough and it got out of hand. They had too

many to control and the tipsters impacted the trust of that advertiser.

Regulation -

- In other markets, such as finance, most companies are FCA regulated, meaning they really have to be careful how they are advertised and portrayed. They must always be clear, fair and not-misleading.
- This means all publishers promoting them must follow the same premise. Most finance companies have strict compliance processes of checking what publishers are saying regularly and not allowing anything to be posted without their prior approval or review.

Big-name brands who've successfully grown their business using superior affiliate programs

Lets now look at some top brands who have grown their affiliate programs to become superior channels for their business.

Plus500:

https://www.500affiliates.com/

Plus500 is one of the largest forex and commodity trading platforms on the web.

Spanning worldwide markets and listed on the stock exchange, they offer one of the most favourable and user-friendly affiliate programs out there...

- Depending on the region they reward commissions of up to $1,000 per customer.
- They offer a 30 day cookie period.
- Always updated creative in industry-standard sizes.

ASOS:

https://ui.awin.com/merchant-profile/5678

ASOS started in the UK and has expanded to North America, Australia and Asia, and has an affiliate program for each market.

ASOS offers over 60,000 items and allows publishers and influencers to benefit from the following...

- Earnings of 5% commission on every sale.
- They offer a 30 day cookie period.
- Updated creative in industry-standard sizes.

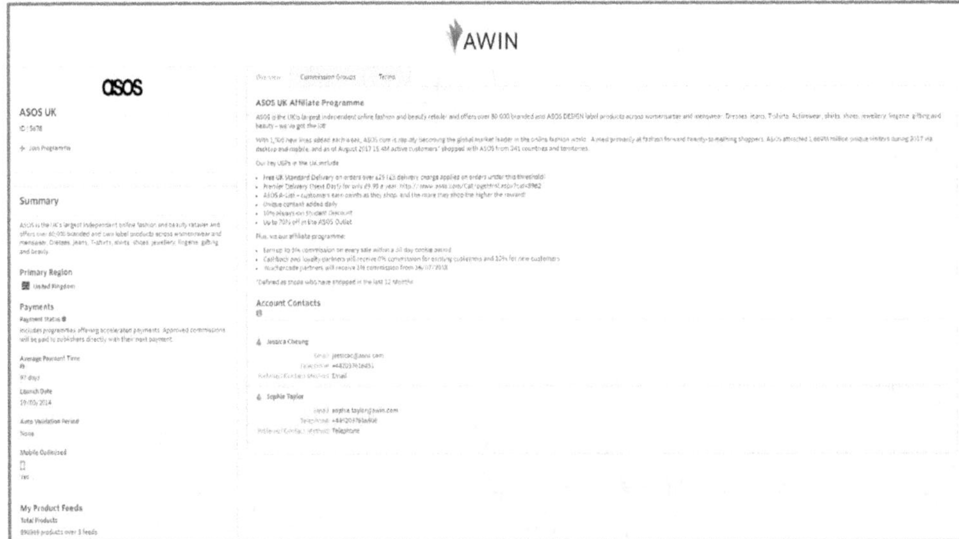

Bet365:

https://www.bet365affiliates.com/

Arguably the largest gambling site in the world, Bet365 has perfected the in-house affiliate programme.

Their success is two-fold...

1. amazing UX
2. ease

Including dynamic creative, as well as favourable commission rates — sometimes even lifetime revenue share!

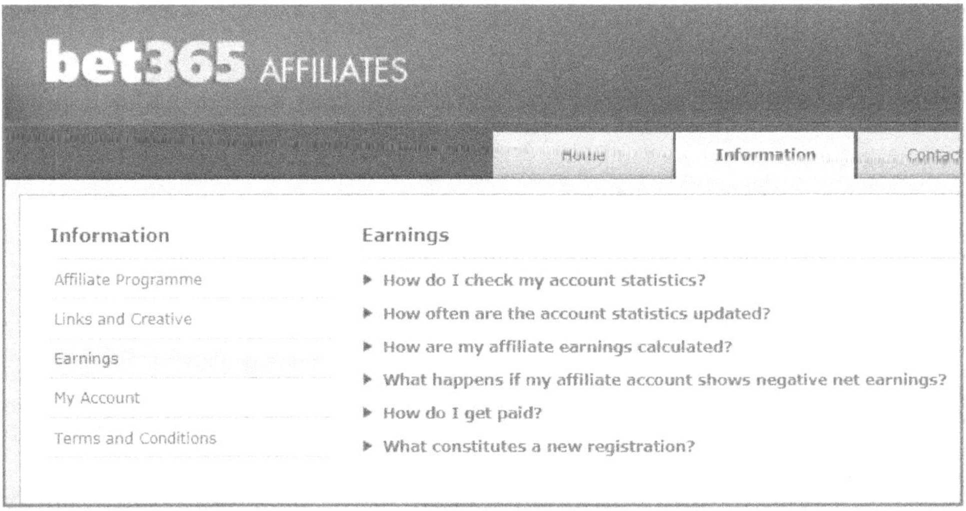

bet365 AFFILIATES

Home | Information | Contact

Information

Affiliate Programme
Links and Creative
Earnings
My Account
Terms and Conditions

Earnings

- How do I check my account statistics?
- How often are the account statistics updated?
- How are my affiliate earnings calculated?
- What happens if my affiliate account shows negative net earnings?
- How do I get paid?
- What constitutes a new registration?

Amazon:

https://affiliate-program.amazon.co.uk/

Most declare this the original and very first affiliate program, some claim they invented online affiliation!

Jeff Bezos was asked one day by book review site if they could promote books sold in his store in turn for a kick back and he obliged - affiliate marketing online was born!

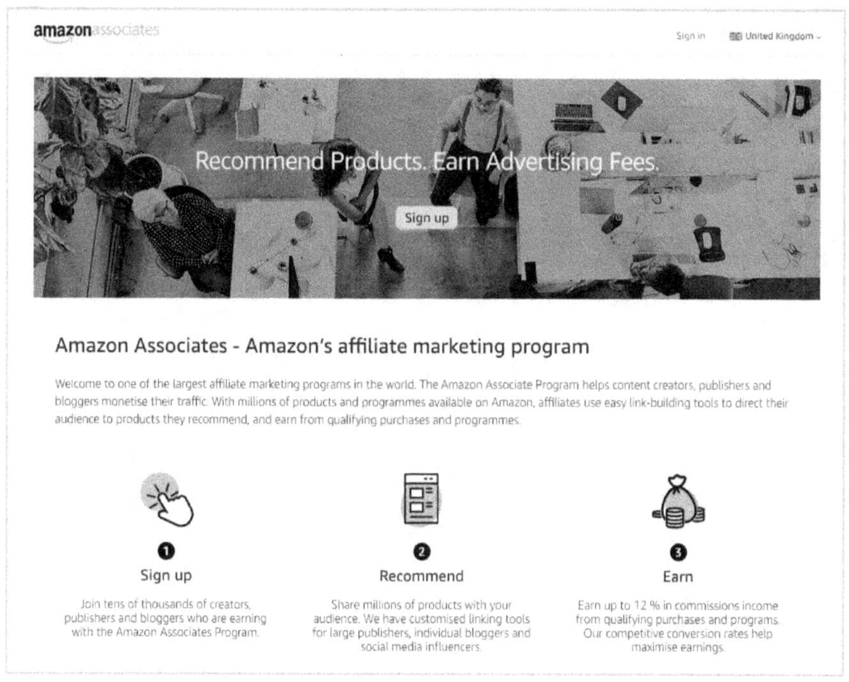

Emma:

https://ui.awin.com/merchant-profile/19791

Emma is an award winning mattress brand that has been making waves in affiliate marketing.

Their tactics often utilise influencers and review sites to gain customers - these affiliate types explain the product and show it in it's best light better than most.

This is also a high ticket item, a mattress can cost £1,000's, so the commission return is very strong and make an attractive proposition to promote for publishers.

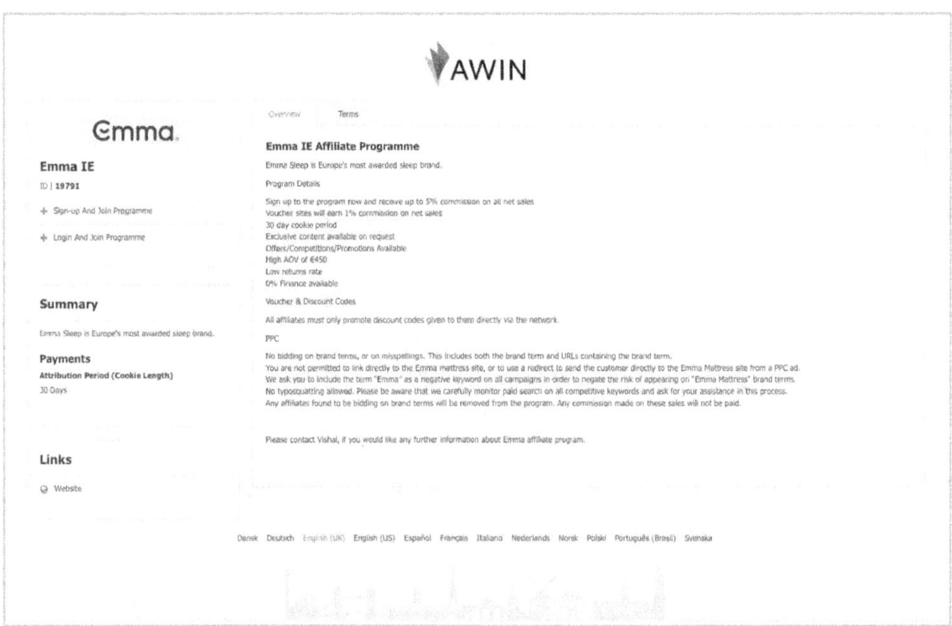

Revolut:

https://www.revolut.com/become-a-revolut-affiliate/

Revolut is one of the fastest growing Fintech companies in the world.

The affiliate program has an in-house homepage but is run by Impact. Payment terms are monthly, and pre-approved assets are provided.

It's a slick affiliate program that encourages publishers to promote their retail and business programs.

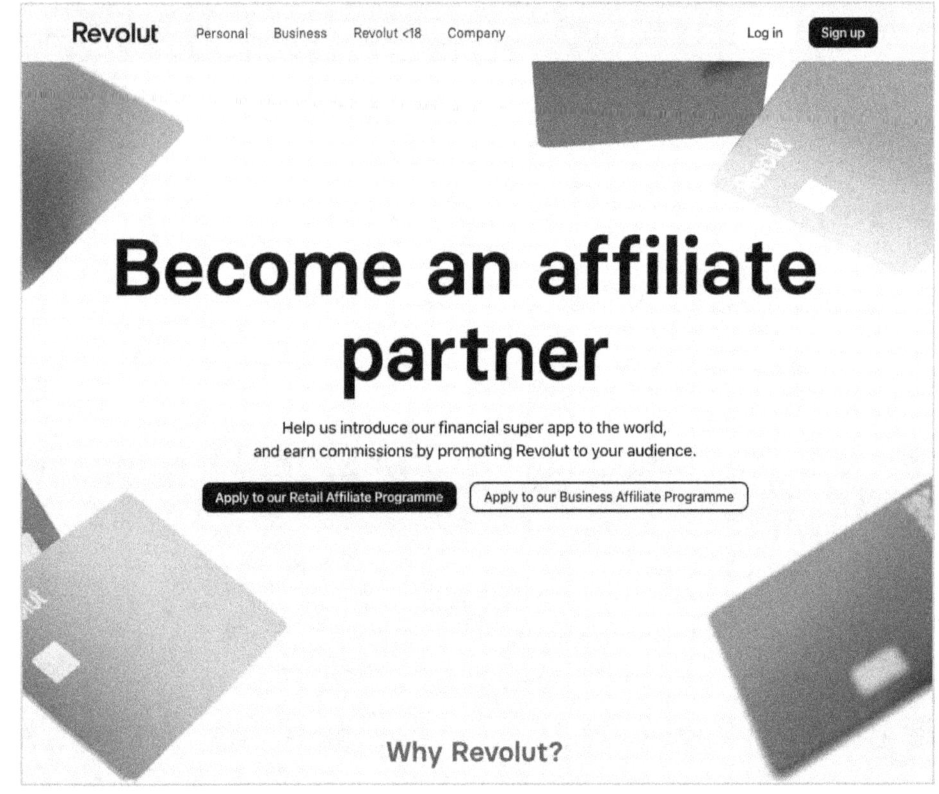

Ongoing Affiliate Strategy

Lastly, now we've covered how to create an Affiliate & Partnerships channel from scratch and grow it in 5 proven steps, the next big area to cover is Affiliate & Partnerships Strategy.

Growing your channel fast is one thing, but sustaining it with continuous growth, as well as maximising the partners you already have, is another.

You can learn all about Affiliate Marketing Strategy in my other book...

'The Complete Guide to Affiliate Marketing Strategy'

Or if you're looking for advice on Affiliate

Recruitment...

'How to find new Affiliates and Partnerships'

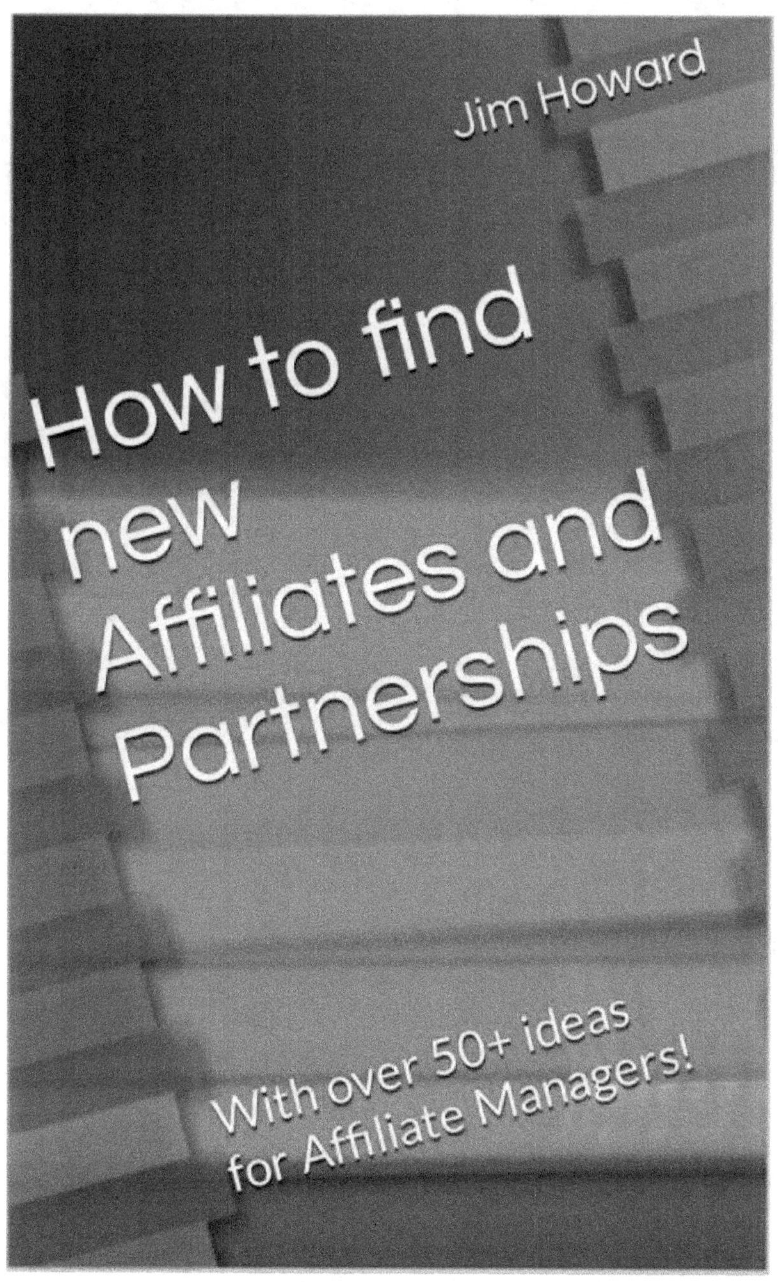

Both you can find on Amazon!

Thank you for reading this book & I hope you found it useful!

If you liked this content you can also...

1. ***Follow us on LinkedIn @GrowPartnerships for the latest partnerships advice & insights***

2. Take our popular Udemy courses:

** The Complete Guide to Partnership Marketing*

(100+ 5 star reviews & rated top 5% of all Udemy courses)

** The Complete Guide to Affiliate Marketing*

(2k+ subscribers & 4.5/5 review score)

Disclaimer

The author takes no responsibility for any misuse of information contained in this book. All information has been taken from actual events and imagery or screenshots from

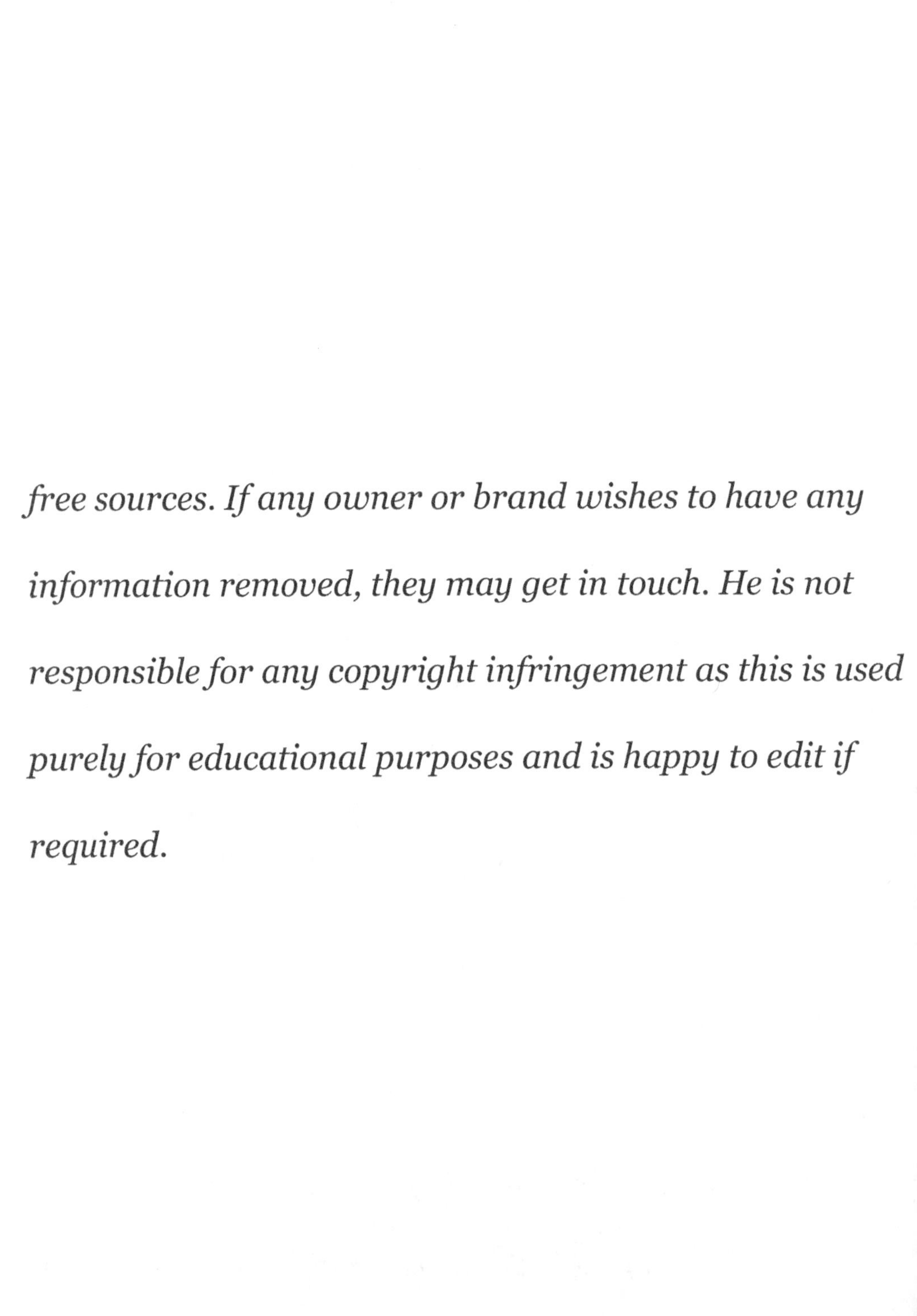

free sources. If any owner or brand wishes to have any information removed, they may get in touch. He is not responsible for any copyright infringement as this is used purely for educational purposes and is happy to edit if required.

www.ingramcontent.com/pod-product-compliance
Lightning Source LLC
LaVergne TN
LVHW010114170826
845678LV00012B/2410